THE GOLDEN DOOR TO RETIREMENT AND LIVING IN COSTA RICA

A guide to inexpensive living in a peaceful tropical paradise

Written by
CRISTÓBAL HOWARD

In collaboration with:
LAMBERT JAMES

THE GOLDEN DOOR TO RETIREMENT AND LIVING IN COSTA RICA

By Cristóbal Howard
With Lambert James

Illustrator: G. Garcia

Sixth Edition

First Edition, published in Costa Rica
Second through Sixth Editions
Published in United States

© 1994-5 M.G. Robinson

ISBN 1-881233-28-6

**Costa Rica Books
P.O. Box 1512
Thousand Oaks, CA 91358**

If there be any splendor in peace, let it rest in a country like this...

The authors.

ACKNOWLEDGEMENTS

This edition would not have become a reality without the invaluable help of many people.

I would first like to thank my typesetter, Debbie Murray, for her hard work and patience.

I am also very grateful to Shirley Miller, the publisher of the *Costa Rican Outlook* newsletter, for her inspiration and guidance during all stages of the development of this latest edition.

A special thanks to Ellen Searby, the author of the best-selling *Costa Rican Traveler*, for giving me the knowledge to open some important doors that have helped my career immensely.

I would also like to thank Anne Becher, Robert Grey and the rest of the staff at Publications in English for believing in me and helping promote my book in Costa Rica.

I am indebted to all the critics whose many favorable reviews made my last edition a success.

Finally, I would like to express my gratitude to my wife and mother for their constant support when I needed it the most.

Chris Howard
San José, Costa Rica
January 18, 1994

ABOUT THE AUTHORS

The author, Christóbal (Chris) Howard and his collaborator, Lambert James, are both fluent Spanish-speaking retirees who have together lived in Costa Rica for over twenty years.

During that time they have had the opportunity to gather a great amount of accurate information related to retirement and living in Costa Rica. Therefore, it is not surprising that they have first-hand knowledge and insight into all aspects of Costa Rica's culture, its people and its government.

This book is based on painstaking research on a variety of related subjects and is the culmination of their collective efforts.

Chris Howard also writes an instructional Spanish language column for one of Costa Rica's English language newspapers.

TABLE OF CONTENTS

CHAPTER IV

KEEPING BUSY IN COSTA RICA   49

CHAPTER V

GETTING AROUND   69

CHAPTER X

FOREWARD

This all-encompassing book is the most concise work available on retirement and living in beautiful Costa Rica. It is intended to orient and familiarize everyone, regardless of age, sex or family size, with the "Little Switzerland of America". To give our readers the most accurate information in the fewest possible words, we have deliberately eliminated extraneous materials that most books of this type usually contain.

Our book is easy to understand. It is intended to be used for reference while you live in comfort for as little as thirty dollars a day or less in Costa Rica. In fact, many Americans who would be considered living below the poverty level in the United States are living like kings in moderate luxury on a modest retirement income in Costa Rica. They are also enjoying one of the best year-round climates in the world (72 degree average in the Central Valley). They live with the generally polite Costa Rican people, who actually like Americans. All this is located only two and one-half hours by air from the United States via Miami or even accessible by car.

Don't be mislead! Other countries, even the good-old USA, are not as safe and relatively crime-free as Costa Rica. This tranquility combined with low prices and the turning back of the clock twenty-years to how things were when the U.S. was unhurried, unspoiled, hassle-free and uncrowded. All things considered, Costa Rica is an ideal place to reside or retire.

Inexpensive medical care, affordable housing, excellent transportation and communication's network, tax incentives, every imaginable activity to stay busy and a government that goes to great lengths to make retirement as easy as possible, combine to make Costa Rica tops on the list of retirement havens.

Costa Rica is the healthiest, safest and most peaceful country south of Canada has a higher life-expectancy and literacy rates than the United States. Furthermore, the January 1993 issue of the magazine *International Living* considered Costa Rica one of the best places on earth to live because of the excellent quality of life. No wonder

TYPICAL OXCART OR *CARRETA*

there are more Americans living in Costa Rica than any other country in Latin American - an estimated 20,000- two thousand of these full-time residents are official retirees or *pensionados*.

In short, Costa Rica has both the warmth and flavor of Mexico, without the anti-Americanism, the physical beauty of Guatemala without a large military presence and the sophistication of Brazil without abject proverty and crime.

It's not too late to join others for what living was made for...PLEASURE. Enjoy this book and thank you for considering and selecting Costa Rica as your place to live. We hope you will find this book interesting, along with discovering new things, as we open the "GOLDEN DOOR" to the best of retirement and living, on a budget everyone can afford NOW!

INTRODUCTION

WELCOME TO BEAUTIFUL COSTA RICA

Costa Rica's friendly three million people, or *Ticos* as they call themselves, invite you to come and experience their tranquil country, with its long and beautiful coastlines, alluring waters of both the Caribbean and the Pacific, pristine beaches and some of the most picturesque surroundings you have ever laid your eyes on. Many visitors say Costa Rica is even more beautiful than Hawaii, and best of all is still unspoiled. Costa Rica has Hawaii's weather without the high prices and offers more beauty and adventure per acre than any other place in the world.

In the heart of the Central Valley, surrounded by beautiful rolling mountains and volcanoes, sits San José, today's capital and largest city in the country. Viewed from above, this area looks similar to some parts of Switzerland or the Lake Tahoe basin on the California-Nevada border.

San José has a mixture of both modern and colonial architecture yet remains charmingly quaint despite being a fairly large city with a slight cosmopolitan flavor. Even though the San José area has a population of around one million people, you always get the feeling you are in a small town, due to the layout of the city.

San José or *Chepe*, as the locals call it, is also the cultural center of the country. It offers good shopping, varied night life, a wide range of hotels, art galleries, theatres, museums, two English newspapers and much more. Finally, because of San José's convenient location any part of the country can be reached in a matter of hours by automobile. We recommend that you use San José as a starting point or home base while you set out to explore Costa Rica and look for a permanent place to live.

CHAPTER ONE

Costa Rica's Land,
History and People

COSTA RICA

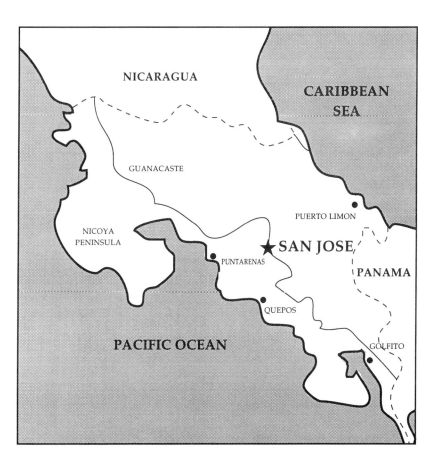

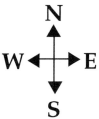

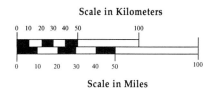

——— Pan American Highway

Scale in Kilometers

Scale in Miles

GEOGRAPHY

Conveniently located in the southern part of Central America Costa Rica occupies a territory of around 20,000 square miles (about the size of the state of West Virginia), including a number of small islands mostly on the Pacific side. It is much like the state of Florida with it's two long coastlines. Because of Costa Rica's large amount of greenery, mountains and forests it has often been compared to both Switzerland and Hawaii. Unlike many areas of Mexico, Central and South America it remains beautiful and warm year-round. This is in part due to its geography and location being bordered on the west by the Pacific Ocean, on the east by the Atlantic Ocean, and having many towering volcanoes on the Central Plateau. Combine all this and you have a unique outdoor tropical paradise.

Lastly, Costa Rica is divided into seven beautiful and geographically different provinces: ALAJUELA, CARTAGO, GUANACASTE, HEREDIA, PUNTARENAS, LIMON and SAN JOSE.

WEATHER

In Costa Rica you will be dressing on the lighter side year-round and enjoy one of the best climates in the world. Temperatures vary little from season to season and are controlled by altitude. The higher you go the colder it gets and the lower you go the warmer it becomes. In the Central Plateau spring-like daytime temperatures hover at around 72 degrees all year, while lower elevations enjoy temperatures ranging from the upper 70's to the high 80's. Temperatures at sea level tend to fluctuate between the high 80's and low 90's in summer with slightly more humidity than at higher elevations.

Like other tropical places, Costa Rica only has two seasons. The summer, or dry season, is generally from about late December to April. The rainy season, or winter as the Costa Ricans call it, runs from around May to November. Unlike many of the world's tropical areas, during the wet season almost all mornings are sunny and clear with only a couple hours of rain in the afternoon. However, the Caribbean Coast tends to be wet all year long. It is for this reason that many foreigners choose to live on the West Coast of Costa Rica. This climate, along with a unique geography, are responsible for Costa Rica's lush vegetation and greenness at all elevations especially during the rainy season.

WHERE TO LIVE IN COSTA RICA

Since we have just discussed Costa Rica's geography and weather, we think now is as good a time as ever to talk about some of the things you should consider before you choose a permanent place to live.

Deciding where to live in Costa Rica depends greatly on your own personal life-style. If you are one of those people who like the stimulation of urban living and spring-like weather all year-long, you will probably be happier living in **San José** or one of the adjacent smaller towns and cities located in the Central Valley. As we mention later in this book in the chapter on keeping busy in Costa Rica, there is a myriad of activities for a retiree in, around and near San José. Retirement is a big change for many people because they find themselves with a lot more free time and sometimes get bored. This should not be a factor if you choose to reside in the San José area because there is a large North American colony and it is always easy to find something to do to keep yourself occupied.

If you don't want to live too far out of town, there are many Americans living in the fashionable suburb of **Rohrmoser**, located on the west-side of the Sabana Park. This area has many beautiful homes of wealthy Costa Ricans and is considered very safe since a large number of well-guarded foreign embassies are located there. There are a few supermarkets, good restaurants, and the new Automercado Shopping Center is located in his area. The only thing bad about Rohrmoser is that bus service is not that good to downtown San José, but you can always take a taxi downtown since they are so affordable.

Another place you might consider living is *Escazú* - a popular suburb where many Americans reside who don't want to live right in town. Escazú is located about five miles west of San José, 10 to 15 minutes driving time via to old two-lane road or new *autopista*, (highway). Escazú is one of the most popular places to live among English speaking foreigners. Bus service is excellent to and from San José. You can catch either a micro-bus or regular bus in the park behind the church in downtown Escazú.

Despite being quaint and country-like, Escazú has pharmacies, mini-malls, supermarkets, excellent private schools, first-class restaurants, trendy shops, a post office, doctors, dentists, and much more. You don't have to go to San José unless you want to. There is also a beautiful private country club and golf course. Housing is plentiful, but expensive, in some areas because of Escazú's popularity among wealthy Costa Ricans, and well-to-do foreigners. However, if you are living on a budget or small pension you can find more affordable housing in the San Antonio de Escazú area. Finally, Escazú's American Legion Post is "the gathering place" for Americans where they can socialize, participate in many activities and make new friends and connections.

Santa Ana, located in the Valley of the Sun, about four miles west of Escazú, is another nice place to live. You can get to Santa Ana by taking the old scenic road from Escazú through the hills, or by the new highway. We recommend you check out this town. It is more rural and less developed than the Escazú area, but there are good supermarkets and some shopping. Lately there has been a building boom in the area. On the minus side, at times bus service can be slow to San José.

La Garita, a pleasant area found west of the airport, is said to have one of the best climates in Costa Rica. There are many foreigners who live in this town. If you can afford the rent or to buy, there are some large homes that come with a good amount of land. We have a friend who rented a home with a pool, a couple of acres of land and a watchman for a very reasonable price. There is also a small zoo and an excellent restaurant called La Fiesta del Maiz found in La Garita. The town of **San Antonio de Belén**, behind the airport and just a couple of miles off the main highway, is also a good place to live. The Ojo de Agua recreational complex is located in this area.

If you desire to combine an urban life-style and seek warmer weather, you can reside in San José's neighboring city **Alajuela**, which is also near the airport. This city is located about 20 minutes by bus from downtown San José. The bus service is excellent during the day, so it is easy to commute to San José if necessary. Because of the warm climate there are many Americans living in Alajuela, so you are bound to make new acquaintances. There are nice parks, movies, restaurants, doctors, supermarkets and more in this city, so it is not necessary to go to San José often. Housing is also very reasonable and plentiful.

Heredia, located at the foot of the Poás Volcano, halfway between San José and Alajuela, is also a nice city. It is only a short distance from San José by car or bus. There don't seem to be as many foreign retirees living in Heredia as in Alajuela, but it is still a good place to live. The surrounding countryside is very beautiful, especially above the city. There is also a university in this city.

Another neighboring city, **Cartago**, found "just over the hill" from San José in the next valley, is not as conveniently located because of the terrain. Perhaps because of the cooler year-round temperatures, fewer North Americans reside there. Bus service is excellent to downtown Cartago from San José because many Costa Ricans who live in Cartago work in San José. The nicest thing about Cartago is its proximity to the beautiful **Orosi Valley**. Viewed from above, this valley is breathtaking. On the floor of the valley there is a large man-made lake, **Cachí**, and park where one can participate in many recreational activities from picnicking to water sports. The lake is fed by the famous **Reventazón** white water-river, that runs through the Orosi Valley.

If you wish to live in a cooler alpine-like setting, you can find nice homes and cabins all over the pine tree covered mountains that surround the Central Valley. Check out the areas around **Monte de La Cruz** and **San José de La Montaña**.

For those of you who seek a more laid back lifestyle, there are also many other small towns and *fincas* (farms) scattered all over the Central Valley. These places are ideal for people who can do without the excitement found in and around large cities.

Zarcero is a quaint little town famous for the sculptured bushes found in front of its church. **San Ramón** is another tranquil town just off the main highway between San José and the port of Puntarenas on the Pacific Coast. **Grecia**, known as the cleanest town in Costa Rica is, a place worth checking out.

Ciudad Quesada, more commonly known as San Carlos, is located north of Grecia. We know a few North Americans who own ranches in this area. Almost everything of importance is found within several blocks of the area surrounding this town's main square.

Northwest of San Carlos is the beautiful man-made **Lake Arenal**. This area is fast becoming popular with foreign residents. The Arenal volcano can often be seen smoking in the distance. Arenal has a lot of potential because of the excellent fishing, sailing, windsurfing and other outdoor activities. There is even a hot spring and resort located in nearby **Tabacón**.

If you are a beach type or warm weather person you have chosen the right country. As you will see in the section on beaches, (Chapter 4), Costa Rica has hundreds of miles of beautiful beaches to chose from.

The Caribbean coast, below **Puerto Limón**, has many places to live. This area particularly appeals to younger people who like beautiful tropical settings, surfing and "reggea music." There is a large colony of foreigners from Europe and the United States living in this area.

The village of **Cahuita**, probably the most popular spot on the Atlantic coast, lies next to Cahuita National Park and has one of the best beaches in the world. **Puerto Viejo**, right down the road, is a great area for snorkeling, surfing and lovers of the Caribbean lifestyle.

About nine kilometers down a dirt road are **Punta Uva**, that has a gorgeous beach for swimming, and the fishing village of **Manzanillo**. This area is spectacular and undeveloped -- but not for long.

As you can see the Caribbean coast sounds very enticing, however, due to an abundant year-round rainfall, most Americans, Canadians and other foreigners chose to live on the often drier West Coast of Costa Rica.

There are many breathtaking beaches all along the Pacific Coast in Guanacate province that are suitable for living. However, many of the surrounding beach communities are either far too tranquil for some people or have too much of a resort atmosphere for others.

Playa del Coco has good night life and there is a small North American contingent living there. **Tamarindo** also has a small foreign colony, but prices of property are very high. **Nosara** is an attractive area to live if you are a nature lover. There is an expatriate community found there. **Montezuma**, a remote little fishing village near the tip of the Nicoya Peninsula, has good beaches and has attracted people from all nations interested in alternative lifestyles.

The Central Pacific Coast also has some superb locations for living. This area has something for everyone with swimming and surfing beaches, excellent sportfishing, as well as developed and undeveloped beaches and natural parks. If you like a lot of action, good waves and partying, we recommend **Jacó Beach**. However, this place may not be to your liking because it gets packed on most summer weekends, holidays and special occasions such as surf tournaments.

The **Quepos-Manuel Antonio** area is considered to be one of the most beautiful places in the world. Most foreigners live in and around the town of Quepos and along the road that leads to **Manuel Antonio National Park**, a few kilometers south and over the hill. **Dominical**, located 42 kilometers south, is a less developed beach area.

In southern Costa Rica, there are some expatriates living around the port of **Golfito**, located on the **Golfo Dulce Bay**. This drab, former banana town leaves a lot to be desired. However, there has been a lot of new development going on recently. Some Americans own large *fincas* (ranches, farms) and others can be found living in more isolated areas around the gulf.

If you do select to live in a beach or rural area, be assured that life is generally less expensive and more laid back than in San José. If you are living on a small budget or pension, you might consider this factor before you choose a permanent place to settle.

In this section we have tried to give you an idea of some of the more desirable places to live in Costa Rica. Since there are so many other great areas to choose from, (it is impossible to describe all of them here), we suggest you read some of the guide books listed in the back of this book to get a better picture of what Costa Rica has to offer. Then you should plan to visit any of the places where you think you may want to live.

COSTA RICA'S UNIQUE HISTORY IN BRIEF

Traditionally Costa Rica has always been a freedom loving country living by democratic rules with respect for human rights.

When Columbus set foot on the Atlantic Coast at a place called Cariari - today this area is called Puerto Limón - he hoped to find vast amounts of gold, so he named this newly found area COSTA RICA — meaning "rich coast" in Spanish. However, unlike Mexico and Peru there were neither large advanced Indian civilizations nor large deposits of gold. The small Indian population offered little resistance to the Spanish and was eventually wiped out by diseases. Faced with no source of cheap labor the Spanish colonists were forced to supply the labor themselves. Thus, a sort of democratic, equitable society developed almost from the beginning with everyone doing their share of the work, and with few people becoming very rich or very poor.

For a long time Costa Rica was almost forgotten by Spain because of the lack of trade and wealth. In fact, Costa Rica became so isolated and unimportant to the mother country that there wasn't even a War of Independence from Spain in the early 1800's, as in the rest of Latin America. Costa Rican's found out about their newly won independence when a letter arrived one month after it was officially granted. This peaceful development continued well into the twentieth-century with only a few minor interruptions. The most notable feature of this process was the abolition of the army forever in 1948.

The military has always posed a constant threat to democratic institutions throughout the rest of Latin America, not to mention turbulent Central America. This is not the case in Costa Rica. What Costa Rica has is a 5,000 man non-political national guard or police force that is under control of the civilian government. Like the police in the United States they concentrate on enforcing the law and controlling traffic.

Because of a lack of military expenditures that go with maintaining an army, Costa Rica has been able to establish one of the best all-encompassing Social Security Systems in the world, an excellent public education system, hospitals, housing, modern communication systems and roads. As a result, Costa Rica has been able to develop the largest proportion of middle class in Latin America and a literacy rate of over ninety-percent. Furthermore, the prohibition of armed forces guarantees political stability and peace for future generations and reaffirms Costa Rica's dedication to the respect for human rights unequaled anywhere else in the world.

GOVERNMENT

Costa Rica's government has been one of the most outstanding examples in the world of an enduring democracy for over forty years. Quite an achievement when one looks at the rest of the world, not to mention Latin America. Being a neutral country Costa Rica has often been compared to Switzerland because of its neutral political posture, with one exception Costa Rica has no army. As we mentioned on the last page, in 1948 Costa Ricans did what no other modern nation has done — they formally abolished their army. Also, the same year they limited the power of their presidents, began universal suffrage, and dedicated their government to justice and equality for all, thus ending discrimination and making Costa Rica a truly unique nation. Consequently, in Costa Rica you don't see any of the racial tension so prevalent in the United States and some other parts of the world. Non-citizens have all the same rights as Costa Ricans. Today there is even a growing woman's rights movement.

COSTA RICA'S FLAG

Costa Ricans set up the legislature, judicial and executive power structure in such a way as to prevent any one person or group from gaining too much power, in order to ensure the continuity of the democratic process. For example, to eliminate the possibility of dictatorships all presidents are limited to one term with **no** possibility of re-election.

Since Costa Rica is such a small country voters can participate more directly in the democratic process. Their votes carry more weight and politicians are more accessible and have more contact with the people. Costa Ricans approach the presidential elections with such enthusiasm that they celebrate election day as if it were one big party or national holiday. In Costa Rica people settle arguments at the ballot box, not on the battle field. It is not surprising that, because of this peaceful democratic tradition, a group of American Quakers established a colony and the University of Peace was started near San José. Finally, Costa Rica's former president, Dr. Oscar Arias Sánchez, was awarded the Nobel Peace Prize in 1987 for his efforts to spread peace and true democracy from Costa Rica to the rest of strife-torn Central America.

THE PEOPLE

Besides having excellent weather and natural beauty, Costa Rica's unique people are probably the country's most important resource and one of the main factors you should consider in selecting Costa Rica as a place to retire. Foreigners who have travelled in Mexico and in other parts of Central America are quick to notice both the racial and political differences between Costa Ricans and their neighbors . Costa Ricans are mostly white and of Spanish origin with a mixture of Germans, Italians, English and other Europeans who have settled in Costa Rica over the years. Argentina and Uruguay are the only other countries in Latin America that have similar racial compositions. There is also a small black population of around 2%, who mainly live on the Atlantic Coast, and a handful of Indians who generally live in the mountainous areas of the Central Plateau and along the Southeastern Coast. Costa Rica has never had a large Indian population like the other countries in the region.

Politically Costa Ricans have always been more democratic than their neighbors --- especially during the last 30 years. Indeed they should be congratulated for being the only people to make true democracy work in such a troubled region. In an issue of National Geographic several years ago, when asked, why Costa Rica isn't plagued by political instability and wars like her neighbors? A Costa Rican replied, in typical Costa Rican humor, or *vacilón*, "We are too busy making love and have no time for wars or revolutions."

Another thing that sets Costa Ricans apart from other countries in the region is the cleanliness of the people. Costa Ricans take pride in their personal appearance. Men, women and children seem to be well dressed. Above all, you don't see as many ragged beggars and panhandlers as in Mexico and many other countries in Latin America.

Costa Ricans are friendly and outgoing and will often go out of their way to help you even if you don't speak Spanish. They are also very pro-American and love anything American like music, TV, fashion and U.S. culture in general. Because of these close ties to the

U.S. and just the right amount of American influence, Costa Ricans tend to be more like North Americans than any other people in Latin America. Surprisingly they also seem to have more liberal attitudes in some areas, especially the young people of the country. This can be due in part to the fact that the Catholic Church has less of a foothold in Costa Rican than in some other Latin American countries.

However, you should not get the wrong idea from reading this, since the vast majority of the people are Catholic and can be conservative when it comes to such issues as movie censorship. Also, Costa Ricans don't miss the chance to celebrate the many religious holidays that occur throughout the year. (See Chapter 9 for a list of some of the most important holidays).

Generally speaking, the people of Costa Rica are fun loving, like to live with "gusto" and know how to enjoy themselves. One only has to go to any local dance hall on a weekend night to see *ticos* out having a good time, or observe entire families picnicing together on any given Sunday – the traditional family day in Costa Rica.

The people of Costa Rica, no matter what their station in life, seem to enjoy themselves with less and do not give as much importance to materialism as North Americans. Even people who can't afford to, seem to be able to eat, drink, be merry and live for today.

Basic old-fashioned family values and unity are very important to Costa Ricans. In fact, the family unit seems to be the most important element in most Costa Rican's lives. Mother's Day is one of the most important holidays. Parents and relatives go to almost any length to spoil and baby their children. Elderly family members are revered and generally treated better than their counterparts in the U.S. and Canada. Costa Rican families will help each other through hard economic times and in the face of poverty. Some foreigners complain that it is difficult to develop deep friendships with Costa Ricans because the family unit is so strong and predominant.

Despite all their great qualities, there is what many people consider a negative side to the character of the Costa Rican people. While being similar to North Americans in many ways and sharing a fondness for some aspects of *"gringo"* culture, make no mistake about it, Costa Ricans are distinctly Latin in their temperament and suffer from many of the same problems endemic to all Latin American societies. Corruption and bribery are a way of life; bureaucratic ineptitude and red-tape are stifling; the concepts of punctuality and logical reasoning are all but non-existent by North American standards, and the "Mañana Syndrome" of leaving for tomorrow what can be done today, at times seems to be the norm rather than the exception. Unfortunately, as in most other countries in Latin America, the custom of *machismo* (manliness) is prevalent to some degree among many Costa Rican males. In case you didn't know, *machismo* is the obsession and constant preoccupation of many Latin men to demonstrate their manliness and show that they are *"macho"* in a variety of ways. Fortunately, the Costa Rican version of *machismo* is more watered down and much milder than the type found in Mexico, but nevertheless still exists.

There is no telling what lengths some men will go to in order to demonstrate their virility. For this very reason many Costa Rican women prefer American men to Costa Rican men because as the Costa Rican women say, "Costa Rican men are *machista* and always have to prove it. You marry a Costa Rican man today and tomorrow he is out chasing other women and drinking!" Speaking of drinking, Costa Rica is reputed to have the highest rate of alcoholism in Central America – an estimated 20% of the population are problem drinkers.

As we discuss in Chapter 4, foreign women walking along the street will be alarmed by the flirtatious behavior and comments that some Costa Rican men make. Many of these flirtations or *piropos*, as they are called in Spanish, may border on obscene but are usually harmless forms of flattery to get a female's attention. Foreign women are best off ignoring this and any other manifestations of *machismo*.

Sadly, some Costa Ricans have misconceptions about North Americans' wealth. There are a few people who seem to think that all Americans and Canadians are millionaires. It is easy to understand why many *ticos* think this way because of the heavy influence of the U.S. television and movies which depict North Americans as being very affluent. Also, the only contact many Costa Ricans have with Americans is primarily with tourists, who are usually living "high on the hog" and spending freely while on vacation. It is therefore not surprising that there are some individuals who will try to take advantage of foreigners by overcharging them for services and goods and others who will use very persuasive means to get you to lend them amounts of money that range from pocket change to even larger sums of money, with no intention of every paying you back. Take our advice and don't lend money to anyone, however convincing their "sob story" seems to be.

You should also know that some foreigners, who have married into Costa Rican families, have been "taken to the cleaners." Because family ties are so strong in Costa Rica and most foreigners are wealthy by Costa Rican standards, you can end up supporting your spouse's whole family. We talked to one retired American who said that he couldn't live on his two thousand dollar a month pension because he had to support not only his wife and step children, but his wife's sister's children as well. Furthermore, he had to lend his father-in-law money to pay off a second mortgage because the bank was going to reposses the latter's house. This is an extreme example, but we have heard many similar stories while living in Costa Rica. Not all Costa Rican families are like the one we just described, but it doesn't hurt to be aware that this situation exists. Be careful with whom you get involved. (See Chapter 4 "Finding Companionship" for more on this subject).

Also, when doing any type of business with Costa Ricans you should excercise extreme caution. A few years ago we had the pleasure of dining with one of the most prominent Costa Rican bankers. We mentioned that we were interested in starting some type of business in Costa Rica to which he replied, "Be very careful when doing business with Costa Ricans. This is not to say that all people are dishonest here. Just be cautious who you deal with."

We suggest that you don't dwell on the negatives we have just mentioned and hope you realize that it is very difficult to generalize or stereotype any one group of people. We are sure that after you have resided in Costa Rica and experienced living with the people, you will be able to make your own judgements. Be assured the good qualities of the Costa Rican people far outweigh any shortcomings they may have. We have included this description of the Costa Rican people because we strongly believe that any book about living in Costa Rica would not be complete without this topic. Finally, to help you understand the Costa Rican people better, we suggest you read the book "The Costa Ricans" that we list in the section of this book titled "Suggested Reading."

CHAPTER TWO

The Economics of
Living in Costa Rica

2.

HOW MUCH DOES IT COST TO LIVE IN COSTA RICA?

One of the most important factors that determine the cost of living for a retiree is life style. If you are a person who is used to all the amenities of a wealthy life style, you are going to spend a lot more than someone who is accustomed to living frugally. But either way, you will still find Costa Rica to be a bargain.

Despite having one of the highest standards of living in Latin America, your purchasing power is much greater in Costa Rica than in the United States or Canada. As you will see in this book, there are many factors that make this statement true.

San José's prices are the second lowest of any city in the Americas, and the cost of goods and services are among the lowest of any city in the world. Housing is only a fraction of the cost that it is in the U. S., and hired help is a steal. Furthermore, utilities such as telephone service, electricity, and water are much lower than in North America. You will never need to heat your home or apartment because of Costa Rica's warm climate, nor will you need to cook with gas, since most stoves are electric. These services will end up costing about 30% of what they do at home. As you know, heating bills in the winter and electricity for air conditioning in the summer can cost hundred of dollars in the states. In addition, public transportation is also very inexpensive. San José and surrounding suburbs occupy a very small area. If you choose to live there, a bus ride across town or to the suburbs usually costs from ten to twenty-five cents. Bus fares to the provinces are also very low (see Chapter 5).

At about a dollar thirty-five per gallon for regular gasoline, Costa Rica's gasoline prices are among the lowest in the Americas. Only oil exporting countries like Mexico and Venezuela have cheaper gasoline. However, you really don't need a car because of the inexpensive public transportation we just mentioned. If you must have a new car to get around or for some other reason, remember new cars are very expensive. Because of this, people tend to hang on to their cars for a long time and take good care of them. We recommend a used car since they are usually in very good condition and their resale value is excellent. As we mention later on food, continuing education, entertainment (movies cost about two dollars) and, above all, health care, are surprisingly affordable.

Once you have lived in Costa Rica for a while, learned the "ins and outs" and made some friends and good contacts, you can cut your living costs even more by doing some of the following: sharing a house or apartment, housesitting in exchange for free rent, investing in high-interest yielding accounts in one of Costa Rica's many banks, working full or part-time (if you can find legal work), starting a small business, bartering within the expatriate community, buying fresh foods in bulk at the Central Market like Costa Ricans do, learning how to get a better rate of exchange on your money, and by even learning Spanish so that you can bargain to get lower prices when you shop.

Taking all of the aforementioned and personal life-styles into consideration, the minimum needed to maintain a decent standard of living for a single person ranges from $600 to $1000 monthly. You can indeed live for as little as $30 a day without reducing your life-style. However, there are single people who scrape by on considerably less and others who spend hundreds of dollars more, again depending on what one is accustomed to. A couple can live well on around $1200 per month, and live in luxury for $2000 a month. Couples with both husband and wife receiving good pensions can live even better. Remember, two can often live as cheaply as one. Any way you look at it, you will enjoy a higher standard of living in Costa Rica and get more for your money when you consider that the average Costa Rican earns only $150-$250 a month.

When you take into account all the above factors plus such intangibles as: good year-round weather, the friendly Costa Rican people, the lack of political strife and serious violent crime (no society is crime free), and a more laid back way of life - no price is too high to pay for living in a unique, tropical paradise like Costa Rica.

Before closing this section, we would like to mention that you should not be alarmed by any high real estate prices that you may hear about or see advertised in either the *Tico Times* or *Costa Rica Today* newspapers. This recent rise in land prices is the result of the current land boom and increasing popularity of Costa Rica. These inflated real estate prices do not reflect the real cost of living in Costa Rica, which is still relatively low when compared to the U.S., Canada and Europe. Even more important, the Costa Rican government has to keep the cost of all basic services and goods affordable for the vast majority of Costa Rican people in order to avoid the social problems that are found in most other Latin American Countries.

Approximate Cost of Living and Prices as of March 1994 in Dollars*

Rentals - Monthly
House (small, unfurnished) $200
House (large, luxurious) .... $1000 - 1200
Apartment (small, 1-2 bedrooms, unfurnished .... $125+
Apartment (large, luxurious) .... $400+
Property Taxes .... $30 a year on a small home

Home Prices (depending on location)
House (small) .... $30,000+
House (large) .... $80,000+

Miscellaneous   Monthly
Electric Bill (apt.) $15-25
Water-Sewage (apt.) $8
Telephone $10
Cable TV $30

Taxi .... .80¢ first kilometer, and .30¢ thereafter per kilometer
Bus Fares (around city) .... .15-.20¢
Gasoline (regular gas) .... $1.25 per gallon
Maid/Gardener .... $1.25 per hour
Restaurant Meal (inexpensive) .... $5.00+

Soda (a diner or coffee shop) Meal $2.00
Restaurant (mid-range) $10.00

Banana .... .5¢
Pineapple $1.00
Papaya .... .70¢
Rice (1lb.) .... .45¢
Steak .... $4.60 lb.
Quart of Milk .... .75¢
Beer .... .50¢ to .75¢
Airmail Letter .... around .30¢ to the U.S.

Doctor's Visit $15-30
Nation Health Insurance ...... $450.00 yearly for permanent residents
New Automobile .... $20,000-$50,000

* These prices are subject to fluctuations at any given time.

• Corporate Resource Consulting firm that compares costs of goods and services, rates San José among the least expensive cities in the world and second to Quito, Ecuador in the Americas.

INVESTING IN COSTA RICA

Let's review just a few of the reasons why Costa Rica has such a magnetism for qualified foreign investors. First, and perhaps most important is the enduring political stability. As you already know Costa Rica has a strong, democratic government dating back to the 1940's without interruption, together with an excellent centralized banking system. Costa Rica is easily accessible from all parts of the world via land, sea or air. Outstanding phone, telex and telegraph systems link Costa Rica internationally to other communications networks. Also, let's not overlook the fact that investors in Costa Rica have equal rights and laws to protect them. Furthermore, there are many opportunities waiting for foreigners to start new businesses that previously have not exsisted in Costa Rica. Finally, as you will see, the cost of labor is cheap.

THE ECONOMICS OF LIVING IN COSTA RICA

Many attractive incentives are available to foreigners to help them invest in Costa Rica. Investments of $50,000 or more in an approved project qualify the investor for legal residency. However, it is not even necessary to become a resident to own or manage a business. Anyone who owns a business can import many items used in the operation of the business and get a tax break on the usual duties. You can contact the incentive section of the **Costa Rican Tourist Institute (I.C.T.)** for more information regarding their incentive programs.

Foreigners can invest in Costa Rica's nationalized banking system, private banks, or finance companies. Interest rates are much higher than in the United States (22% or even higher) and there are many attractive savings accounts and time deposit programs to choose from. There are some degrees of bank secrecy, liberal money transfer regulations and favorable tax laws for foreigners (see the section in this chapter titled "Taxes").

Foreigners can also invest in the local Stock Exchange (**Bolsa Nacional de Valores**) to get better returns than from tradition financial systems.

There are around twenty firms registered with the National Stock Exchange. Costa Rican stock brokers can study economic trends and give you advice on investing in government bonds, real estate, time deposits and other investments.

The Costa Rican Stock Exchange is regulated by the National Securities Comission, which is the counterpart of the U.S. Securities and Exchange Comission. They can give you information about the reliability of firms and brokers.

If you are seriously interested in investing in Costa Rica, we suggest that you try to get a copy of "The Investors Guide to Costa Rica" which is available through the **Costa Rican-American Chamber of Commerce or AMCHAM.** There is also a monthly magazine available titled "Business in Costa Rica" that also has advice on how to invest in Costa Rica.

For additional information contact:
American Chamber of Commerce of Costa Rica-AMCHAM
P.O. Box 4946-1000
San José, Costa Rica
Tel: 011-506-233-1133; Fax: 001-506-223-2349

Coalition for Investment Initiatives-CINDE
P.O. Box 7170-1000
San José, Costa Rica
Tel: 011-506-220-0036; Fax: 011-506-220-4750
Export Promotion Center - CENPRO
P.O. Box 5418-1000
San José, Costa Rica
Tel: 001-506-220-0066; Fax: 011-506-223-5722
The Costa Rican Stock Exchange
Bolsa Nacional de Valores
P.O. Box 1756
San José, Costa Rica
Tel: 011-506-222-8011; Fax: 011-506-255-0531
National Securities Commission
P.O. Box 10058
San José, Costa Rica
Tel: 011-506-233-2840; Fax: 011-506-233-0969
Canada Costa Rica Chamber of Commerce
Tel: 257-3241

TIPPING

On all hotel bills a 10% sales tax is charged as well as a 3% tourist tax. In cafes and restaurants there is a 10% tip and a 10% tax included. So tipping above that amount is not necessary. Of course, employees such as bellhops and taxi drivers are appreciative of any additional gratuity for excellent service.

INEXPENSIVE HOUSING

Housing is both affordable and plentiful in Costa Rica. With the exception of downtown San José, rents for houses or apartments are very reasonable -- about half the cost of the United States or less. Depending on location and personal taste, a small house or large apartment can usually be rented for a few hundred dollars per month. A luxurious house or apartment will go for $600 to $1000 per month or even higher. When you figure that most Costa Ricans pay way less than $150 monthly for rent, a few hundred dollars for rent should get you a nice place to live. Most houses and apartments have all the amenities of home: large bedrooms, bathrooms with hot water, kitchens, dining rooms, a laundry room and even maid's quarters since help is so inexpensive in Costa Rica.

For those of you who can't afford a house in the states, home prices start at around $30,000 with financing available. Unlike Mexico some beach front property may be purchased. However, you can no longer buy or build within 200 meters from the high tide line except when there is some type of existing housing or new tourism project involved. This 200 meter area is called the *Maritime Zone* or *Zona Marítima* in Spanish. There are also condominiums, farms, lots and ranches for sale at bargain prices depending on their location. You will be pleased to know that there are no capital gains taxes on real estate in Costa Rica making it an excellent investment. You do have to pay some yearly taxes but they are very low by U.S. standards.

If you decide to buy some type of real estate you should know that an attorney is necessary to do the legal work for purchasing properly. We strongly recommend that your lawyer do a thorough search of all records before you make your purchase and make sure that there are no encumbrances (*gravámenes*) on it. You can find out any information about property at the *Registro de Propiedades* (sort of like our recorder's office) in the suburb of Zapote, located about five minutes from downtown San José by car or taxi.

Before you buy property, your lawyer should explain the legalities of buying and selling property in Costa Rica. **Be sure not to hire the same lawyer used by the seller of land**. Also, don't forget to check if you are buying the land from its rightful owner. Some owners have been known to sell the land to several buyers. You can protect your potential real estate investment further if you: talk with neighbors about water shortages, safety and burglaries in the area; always see the property in person and don't buy sight unseen; make sure that there are no problems with squatters; check to see if you need special permits to build; check the comparative land values in your area to see if you are getting a good deal, and make sure that roads, electricity and telephone service are available if you are thinking of living in a remote area. If you can't live on your property year-round, then you will have to have a guard or a reliable housesitter to watch it for you.

Also, we suggest that you rent for at least six months. Make sure to buy in an area were it is easy to rent or sell your home or condominium, in case you have to change your plans or in the event of a personal emergency.

To find an apartment, house or to purchase land look for listings in the *Tico Times* newspaper or inquire at one of the many real estate or rental agencies located in downtown San José. Better yet, talk to other retirees. If you want to save money you should look in the local Spanish newspapers *La Nación* or *La República* because prices are usually lower. You should also keep in mind that housing costs are much higher in *gringo* enclaves like Escazú and Rohrmoser. Also, be sure to keep in mind that the farther away you live from San José and other cities you will be able to get much more for your money.

In Costa Rica you can even build your retirement dream house if you so desire since land, labor and materials are all inexpensive. However, you might want to think twice about undertaking a project of this type, because you could be flirting with disaster. Many retirees, who have built homes complain that it sounds easier than it really is and would not do it again because of many costly delays, somewhat unreliable labor, fussy building inspectors, different laws and building codes and many other unforseen problems. It is best to talk with other foreigners who have built homes to see what obstacles they encountered. Finally, we suggest that you read the book about investing in real estate by Bill Baker the we list in the appendix.

AFFORDABLE HIRED HELP

As you already know full-time, as well as part-time domestic help, are both hard to find and prohibitively expensive in the United States for the average person, not to mention a retiree. This is not the case in Costa Rica. The cost for a live-in maid or other full-time help usually runs between $150 and $200 per month. Often you can hire a couple for a bargain price with the woman working as a maid and the man working as a full-time gardener and watchman. In Costa Rica a maid usually does everything from washing clothes to taking care of small children. You can also use your maid to stand in line for you, run errands and bargain for you in stores since foreigners often end up paying more for some items because of their naivity and lack of language skills. General handymen and carpenters are also inexpensive. If you are infirm, one of the above people can assist you with many other daily tasks. To find quality help check with other retirees for references or look in local newspapers. (*The Tico Times*, La *República or La Nación*).

THE ECONOMICS OF LIVING IN COSTA RICA

Costa Rica's labor laws for domestic workers are very strict and rather difficult to interpret. All domestic employees have the right to social security benefits from the *Caja Costarricense de Seguro Social* (roughly the equivalent of our Social Security System). This important institution pays for sick leave, general health care, disability pensions and maternity care.

It is important for you to know that it is the employers responsibility to pay monthly social security payments for each employee. The employer must make monthly payments of about 20 percent of the workers monthly wages. In return the worker is entitled to all of the social security systems services mentioned above. New employees must be registered with the social security within a week of being hired. All new employees must register in an office located downtown (Tel: 223-9890).

Employers must also pay minimum wage to employees. This wage is set by the Ministry of Labor (Tel: 223-7166) and depends on the job and skills required. Wages average about $100 per month. Live-in help can receive an additional 50% more that is not actually paid to them each month but is used when computing certain benefits and bonuses.

Domestic help who live in your home cannot be required to work more than twelve hours a day, although nobody expects this. Live-in workers usually end up working eight hours a day like other workers. Most regular employees work an eight hour day, five days per week. Live-in employees can work more than this but have to be given some time off.

Furthermore, employees are entitled to a paid vacation depending on their length of employment and whether or not they are full or part-time.

Employers must also pay an *aguinaldo* or Christmas bonus if an employee has worked from December 1 through November 30. It is the equivalent of one month's salary. This Christmas bonus should be paid in early December. Don't forget that live-in employees receive an additional 50 percent Christmas bonus.

A maternity leave of one month before a baby's birth is required with the employee receiving 50% of her normal salary.

In some cases it is the employer's responsibility to pay severance pay and all accumulated, unused vacation time when a worker is terminated, the proportionate *aguinaldo* and any wages due. An employee must also be given notice prior to being laid off. Severance pay is usually one month's salary for each year worked. If an employee resigns voluntarily, the employer doesn't have to pay severance pay. For your information, severance pay is called *prestaciones*.

We have only briefly touched on the main points of Costa Rican labor law because it is very complex. If you have any questions we advise you to contact the Minister of Labor (223-71-66) or better yet your attorney. It is best to have your lawyer help you with any labor related matters to avoid unnecessary problems that might arise between you and your hired help.

MEDICAL CARE

Costa Rica has an up-to-date, affordable health care system with hospitals, clinics and complete medical services in all major cities and some towns. Costa Rica has been considered by numerous international medical authorities as having one of the best, low-cost health care systems in the world when considering preventive and curative medicine. The infant mortality rate is lower in Costa Rica than in the United States, and life expectancy rates are as high if not higher. Cosmetic surgery is inexpensive and Costa Rica's plastic surgeons are among the world's best. Laboratories and equipment are first class. You can feel safe having most types of operations without returning to the U.S. or Canada. Most of these procedures only cost a fraction of what they do in the U.S. For instance, a heart bypass operation only cost a few thousand dollars in Costa Rica.

Public medical facilities are so good that you don't usually have to resort to private care since most private specialists are required by law to work part-time in public hospitals. However, private clinics and hospitals do provide quicker services. In the event that you have to enter a private hospital, costs will generally be well under a hundred dollars a day. We might point out that this includes your own spacious private room and bathroom, usually a T.V. and an extra bed or sofa-bed so that a relative may spend the night, if necessary.

We know an American who spent a couple of days in the private Clínica Católica hospital and said, "The attention was first class, the food was as good as home cooking and the same care would have cost thousands of dollars in the states." It is important to know that payment can be made at most hospitals and clinics with any major credit card. Foreign medical insurance is not accepted, but you can get a reimbursement from you own health insurance company, if they cover you abroad.

Most Costa Rican doctors are excellent and have been trained in Europe, the United States or Canada. If you don't speak Spanish, you don't have to worry since many local doctors speak English, however, most receptionists and nurses do not. Doctor's fees for office visits vary. A good private specialist usually charges between $15 and $30 per visit, with some doctors charging a little more and others a little less. Better yet, if you join Costa Rica's national health care system you don't have to pay for each office visit, only a small monthly membership fee. Dentists are also very reasonable and only charge a fraction of what their counterparts do in the states. On the average, dental work costs about 25%-30% less than in the U.S. and more expensive procedures even less. The quality of this dental work done in Costa Rica is equal to that done in the U.S., Canada or Europe.

If you have any questions about medical fees or doctors you can consult the Colegio de Médicos, which is the Costa Rican equivalent of the AMA. To find a good English speaking physician or specialist talk to other retirees, look in the Yellow Pages under *Médicos* or look for doctor's ads in the *Tico Times*.

Costa Rica's health care system is available to retirees (*pensionados*) and other foreign residents. They may join the **Caja Costarricense de Seguro Social** (Costa Rican Social Security System) and enjoy free medical attention like most Costa Ricans do. They can also enroll their entire family for as little as thirty dollars monthly. Retirees need not worry about lacking adequate medical coverage outside the United States.

There is also a new type of medical insurance being offered through the Association of Retirees, to supplement the government's Social Security System. This plan is excellent. For a few hundred dollars a year a man or woman between 50 - 70 can get a yearly coverage of almost $35,000. This program, in conjunction with the government Social Security System, should provide more than ample medical coverage especially when you consider the low cost of health care in Costa Rica.

While checking out Costa Rica as a tourist, to see if it is the place for you to settle, you can get temporary medical insurance through the Costa Rican Social Security office and the **International Organization of Cultural Interchanges (O.I.C.I.)** This insurance may be bought at many travel agencies, language schools or tourism offices. If you plan to reside in the country for more than one month and your tourist visa and other papers are up to date, contact the O.I.C.I. office located on he fourth floor of the Mendiola building on Avenida Central, or call 222-7867.

Pharmacies are plentiful in Costa Rica and stock most standard medicines available in the United States, Canada and Europe. There are even some that remain open 24-hours a day, conveniently located in downtown San José at the **Clínica Bíblica Hospital**, 223-64-22, and at the **Clínica Católica Hospital** 225-90-95, and at the **Clínica Santa Rita**, 221-64-33. The **Fischel** pharmacy, located across from the main post office in San José, is open 24-hours a day, sometimes has a doctor on duty for medical advice and will deliver medicine and prescriptions in the San José area. Speaking of pharmacies, many medicines available only by prescription in the U.S. may can be purchased over-the-counter at any local *"Farmacia."* In Costa Rica pharmacists are permitted to prescribe medicines as well as administer on-the-spot injections. In general, most medicines cost 50% or less of what they do in the United States.

In Costa Rica there is also full service custodial health care available for the elderly (men and women alike) at a very low cost. Care for less independent senior citizens can be found for around $1000 per month. Retirements Centers International offers comprehensive medical care and assistance which includes all medicines, lab work, dental care, physical therapy, rehabilitation and special diets etc. These programs are some of Central America's best and considerably less expensive than in the United States. However, even if these facilities are beyond an elderly person's means, a full-time live-in domestic worker can be hired in the capacity of a nurse for a couple of hundred dollars monthly. In addition to caring for an infirm person this worker can tend to other household chores.

For additional information contact:

RETIREMENT CENTERS INTERNATIONAL
Apdo. 2627-1000 San José, Costa Rica, Central America
Telephone (506) 222-10-55

HOGAR RETIRO PARA ANCIANOS SAN PEDRO
Apdo. 52250, Tres Rios, Costa Rica

HOTELES GERIATRICOS
Apdo. 2140-100, San José, Costa Rica

HOGAR DE ANCIANOS PEDRO CLAVER
Apdo. 441, San José, Costa Rica

GOLDEN VALLEY HACIENDA
Telephone: 443-85-75

VILLA CONFORT GERIATRIC
Telephone: 443-81-91
* Once again, to find a good physician or specialist talk to other retirees, look in the yellow pages under *"MEDICOS"* or look for doctor's ads in the *Tico Times* and *Costa Rica Today.* Below are the names of some Engilish speaking physicians and dentists.

Dr. Manuel Trimiño Vásquez - Pysician/Psychiatrist.
Tel: (506)221-61-40

Dr. Ronald Pino - Plastic Surgery.
P.O. Box 447-1007 San José, Costa Rica.
Tel: (506) 220-02-24 Fax: (506) 231-60-17.

Dr. Ronald H. De Pass Jimenez - Family Dentistry.
P.O. Box 2463-1000, San José, Costa Rica.
Tel: (506) 228-9933 Fax: (506) 228-99-31

Dr. Rudolf Nuñez - Clinical Dermatology.
Tel: (506) 222-62-65 Fax: (506) 257-02-44

Dr. Willy Feinzaig - Urology.
P.O. Box 110-1000, San José, Costa Rica
Tel: (506) 222-10-10 Fax: (506) 231-28-67

Dr. Alejandro Lev - Plastic Surgery.
P.O. Box 183-1007, San José, Costa Rica
Tel: (506) 221-83-29

Dr. Joaquín Martínez - Ophthalmologist.
Tel: (506) 289-74-18 Fax: (506) 238-0005

Dr. Arnoldo Fournier - Plastic Surgery
P.O. Box 117-1002, San José, Costa Rica
Tel: (506) 222-51-60 Fax: (506) 255-43-70

Dr. Norma Kaminsky - Acupuncture.
Tel: (506) 222-51-60

Dr. John Anastasi P. - Chiropractor.
Tel: (506) 231-31-65

FINDING WORK IN COSTA RICA

We have some not too encouraging news for those of you who are living on a small pension and hope to supplement your income by finding some type of employment, or for other retirees who need to work just to keep busy. Finding work can be very difficult, but not impossible. In the first place, it is not easy for a Costa Rican, not to mention foreigners who don't speak fluent Spanish, to find permanent work. If you happen to be one of the few foreigners who is lucky enough to have mastered Spanish, you will probably have a better than average chance of finding some type of work in tourism or some other related field. However, your best bet may be to try to find employment with a North American firm that does business in Costa Rica. You may be able to land some type of job as a salesman or a representative.

Even if you know little or no Spanish, you have a some chance of finding work as an English teacher at one of the many language institutes in San José. But don't expect to earn more than a survival salary from one of these jobs because the minimum wage in Costa Rica is very low. Working as a full-time language instructor you can't expect to make more than a few hundred dollars monthly. As a supplemental source of income this is fine, but you won't be able to live on it, given the kind of life style you are probably used to.

You can also try putting one of your skills to use by providing some type of service to the large expatriate community in Costa Rica. For example, if you are a writer or journalist you might be able to find work at one of Costa Rica's two English language newspapers. Unfortunately, if you are a retired professional such as a doctor or lawyer you can't practice in Costa Rica because of certain restrictions but there is nothing stopping you from offering your services as a consultant to other foreigners and retirees.

As if it were not hard enough to find work in Costa Rica, a work permit or residency is required of all foreigners before they can work legally. Labor laws are very strict and the government doesn't want foreigners taking jobs away from Costa Ricans. You are only allowed to work if you can do some type of specialized work that a Costa Rican can't do. However, many foreigners work under the table without a work permit. This practice is illegal, but you do so at your own risk if you want to bear the consequences. If you don't seek remuneration, you can always find some type of volunteer work to keep busy. This kind of work is legal, so you don't need a work permit or run the risk of being deported for working illegally. Also, as a foreigner you can invest in Costa Rica and even start your own business with only some restrictions.

As we stated earlier in this chapter, Costa Rica is ripe for those innovative foreigners that are willing to take a risk and start businesses that have not previously existed. We might add, however that running a business in Costa Rica is not like managing a business in the United States because of unusual labor laws, the Costa Rican work ethic and the Costa Rican way of doing business.

If you do choose to establish your own business, keep in mind that you are in some cases limited to managerial or supervisorial duties and will have to hire Costa Ricans to do the bulk of everyday work. We also recommend that you take the time to do a thorough feasibility study, you don't assume that what works in the U.S. will be successful in Costa Rica. Check out restrictions and the tax situation. And most important, choose a business in which you have a lot of prior experience.

After reading the above, if you still have some questions or are confused, we advise you to consult a knowledgeable Costa Rican attorney for further information.

MONEY

The *colón*, named for Christopher Columbus, is Costa Rica's official currency. Despite being one of the most stable currencies in Latin America, it has recently been somewhat shaky because of devaluations. Fortunately, the devaluations are relatively small when compared to the mega-devaluations and run-away inflation rampant in other Latin American countries. Since your main source of income will probably be in dollars, you should not worry too much about devaluations unless you have large amounts of money in *colones*, which is not advisable for long-term investments. Devaluations can be good because they increase your purchasing power until prices catch up. The rate of exchange, which is set by the Central Bank, as of December 1993 was around 150 colones per dollar.

BLUE BILLS	¢5000
RED BILLS	¢1000
PURPLE BILLS	¢500
GRAY BILLS	¢100
LIGHT GREEN BILLS	¢50
BROWN BILLS	¢20
COINS	c20,c10,5,2-1 colones

You can exchange your money at most banks between 9 a.m. and 4 p.m., Monday through Friday. If you have to exchange money at a bank, do so early in the morning because lines can be very long later in the day and you can end up waiting for what seems to be an eternity. You should always carry your passport or *pensionado* I.D. when exchanging money or for other banking transactions. When banks are closed you can change money at a special changing office located in downtown San José under the Plaza de la Cultura, open Saturday 9 a.m. to 3 p.m. and on Sundays, 9 a.m. to 1 p.m., and on some holidays. Also, most hotels can change certain amounts of travelers checks or dollars.

Money can also be changed on the black market where you may get a more favorable rate of exchange than in the banks. Black market money changers can be found along Avenida Central between Calles 2 and 4, in the vicinity of the Post Office. You don't have to look for these money changers since they will usually approach you. Many people prefer to change their money this way because all transactions are quick and there are no lines as in the banks. Once you have been in Costa Rica for a while some of these money changers will get to know you and end up doing the majority of your transactions.

Be careful of slick change artists who may be distributing counterfit bills.

There are some money changers who work more discretely out of their own offices in the same area of town. We recommend the **Villalobos Brothers Money Traders**, who have a large clientele of retirees and other foreigners. In addition to changing money, they cash personal and social security checks and provide many other related services. Their office is located 75 meters south of the main

Post Office next to the Banco Lyon, on the second floor of the Schyfter Building. Tel: (506) 233-00-90/233-31-27. Fax: 223-88-38.

BANKING

There are branches of Costa Rica's banks located in San José and other large cities and towns. The headquarters of Costa Rica's largest banks **El Banco Nacional, El Banco de Costa Rica** and **El Banco Central** are located in downtown San José near the Central Post Office. It is advisable to open some type of account at one of these banks, so that you can have a dollar account to protect against unexpected currency devaluations, cash personal checks, obtain a safety deposit box for some of your valuables and facilitate having money sent to you from abroad. Regarding the latter, you should make sure that the bank you choose works in conjunction with a U.S. correspondent bank to avoid untimely delays in cashing checks. **Warning:** You should never plan to do any banking on either the second or last Friday of the month since most Costa Rican workers are paid on these days and lines sometimes extend outside the bank.

TAXES

You will be pleased to know that as far as taxes are concerned there are many advantages to residing in Costa Rica. Investors pay no capital gains taxes on real estate investments in Costa Rica. High interest bearing bank accounts are also tax free. It is interesting to note that the maximum Costa Rican tax rate is around 30% with no city or state taxes and very low property taxes. Furthermore, you can form a Costa Rican "offshore" corporation, called a *Sociedad Anónima*, to shelter your earnings.

Briefly a *Sociedad Anónima* is a type of anonymous corporation you can set up without your name appearing on any records. You control all the stock in the corporation but your identity remains unknown. This enables you to maintain some degree of secrecy in your financial matters If you are seriously thinking about forming one of these anonymous corporations, we suggest you contact your attorney. Your lawyer can explain how these corporations work as well as their advantages and disadvantages.

If you go into business and choose to form one of these tax sheltered corporations all of your expenses can be written off. Also, unlike some other places, a foreign retiree is not required to pay Costa Rican taxes on his external income (income generated abroad). So, you can see why Costa Rica is considered a tax-haven by many people. As far as U.S. income tax is concerned, you must file your U.S. income tax returns yearly through the American Embassy. You have to declare all income earned abroad. U.S. citizens living abroad, may claim a tax exemption for up to $70,000 on overseas earned income. Fortunately, if you reside outside the U.S. you don't have to file your taxes until June 15th.

If you have any tax questions, contact the U.S. Embassy or IRS. You can call either the Consular Section of the U.S. Embassy, 220-39-39 or the nearest IRS office in Mexico City at (525) 211-0042, ext. 3557.

If you need help with your tax forms and returns while living in Costa Rica, contact the local H&R Block, Tel: 231-1004. You can also call Gordon Finwall, a tax attorney and C.P.A. living in Costa Rica, at 224-1351 or another C.P.A., David Houseman at 223-2787 or 239-2045, for income tax assistance or to obtain help with IRS problems.

Canadians should contact the local Canadian Consulate at 255-35-22 if they need information about their tax obligations while living abroad.

INSURANCE

While living in Costa Rica you will find all types of insurance much more reasonable than in the United States. Auto, fire and theft insurance will usually end up costing less than half of what they do in the States. If you own an automobile, Costa Rican insurance is compulsory and paid for when your car is registered. This mandatory liability insurance is called *Seguro Obligatorio*.

We have already mentioned the affordability of medical insurance in Costa Rica in the section titled "Medical Care." The *Instituto National de Seguros* or *INS*, as it is called, will handle all of your insurance needs. However, because not everyone's insurance needs are the same and laws and coverages work differently in Costa Rica, we suggest you consult your attorney or the English speaking insurance agent we have listed below:

Garrett y Asociados, S.A.

Apartado 5478-1000

San José

Tel: 233-24-55; 272-00-07

CHAPTER THREE

Education

LEARNING SPANISH

Although a large number of Costa Rica's well-educated people speak English, (there are more than 20,000 English-speaking foreigners living permanently in Costa Rica) Spanish is the official language. Anyone who seriously plans to live or retire in Costa Rica should have some knowledge of Spanish — the more the better. Frankly, you will be at a disadvantage, somewhat handicapped and probably always be considered a foreigner to some degree, without Spanish. Part of the fun of living in another country is to be able to communicate with the locals, make new friends and be able to enjoy the culture. Speaking Spanish will enable you to achieve these ends, have a much more rewarding life style and open the door for many new and interesting experiences. Knowing some Spanish can also save you some money when you do your shopping and, in some cases, can keep people from taking advantage of you.

For those of you who take our advice and choose to study Spanish in a formal setting, for a modest fee you can enroll at one of the intensive conversational language schools located around San José. In addition to language instruction, most of these schools offer exciting field trips, interesting activities and room and board with local families — all of which are optional. Living with a family that speaks little or preferably no English is one of the best ways to improve your language skills, make new friends and learn about Costa Rican culture at the same time.

Spanish is not a difficult language to learn. With a little self-discipline and motivation, anyone can acquire a basic Spanish survival vocabulary of between 200 - 3000 words in a relatively short period of time. Many Spanish words are similar enough to English, so that you can figure out their meanings by just looking at them. The Spanish alphabet is almost like the English one, with only a few minor exceptions. Pronunciation is easier than English because you say words like they look like they should be said. Spanish grammar is somewhat complicated, but can be made easier if you are familiar with English grammar and find a good Spanish teacher. Practicing with native speakers is perhaps the best way to improve your Spanish because you can hear how Spanish is really spoken in everyday conversation. You will learn many new words and expressions ordinarily not found in your standard dictionary.

Watching Spanish television, listening to the radio and language cassettes can also improve your Spanish. Speaking of cassettes, we also suggest that if you are a beginner or have little knowledge of spoken Spanish, you purchase the one-of-a-kind *Costa Rican Spanish Survival* book and accompanying cassette advertised in this book. It is designed especially for people planning to retire or live in Costa Rica and makes learning easy because the student learns the natural way, by listening and repeating like a child without grammar. However, if you are interested in a more in-depth study of Spanish we are including a list of language schools at the end of this section. We suggest you first check with the school of your choice for current prices.

The type of Spanish spoken in Costa Rica is basically the same as standard Castillian Spanish except for one big difference that is likely to confuse the beginning student. In Spanish there are two forms used when addressing a person: The polite form, *USTED*, and the informal form, *TU*. However, this is not the case in Costa Rica. In Costa Rica the form *VOS* is used instead of the more traditional form of *TU*. The verb form used with *VOS* is formed by changing the *r* at the end of a verb infinitive to *s* and adding an accent to the last syllable. This form is seldom taught because it is considered a colloquial form, only used in Central America and some parts of South America (Argentina and Uruguay) and is not found in most Spanish textbooks.

Don't worry! Once you live in Costa Rica for a while and have a chance to get used to the Costa Rican way of speaking Spanish you will learn to use the *VOS* form almost automatically. If you do make a mistake and use the *TU* form, most Costa Ricans will overlook it because they know you are not a native speaker. Costa Ricans will

LIMITED OFFER

Learn to Speak Spanish Like a Costa Rican.

Costa RicanSpanish Survival Book & Cassette

This course is a must for those who wish to gethe most out of Costa Rica and be able to communicate effectively with the people. It is a process of learning by listening and repeating without boring, tiresome grammar. It has already helped thousands of people master the basics of Spanish in real life situations.

- COSTA RICAN IDIOMS

- CORRECT PRONUNCIATION

- USEFUL EVERYDAY EXPRESSIONS

- PRACTICAL VOCABULARY

- PROVEN NATURAL METHOD

- GUARANTEED RESULTS

- POCKET SIZE FOR TRAVEL

Course Material is Pocket Size -- Ideal For Travel

ORDER TODAY

ADDITIONAL CASSETTES $4.99 each
ADDITIONAL BOOKS $7.99 each

SEND CHECK OR MONEY ORDER TO:

BOOK AND CASSETTE
REGULAR $12.95 set
NOW $10.95 set
+ 2.95 handling

$13.90 set

**M. ROBINSON
P.O. BOX 1512
THOUSAND OAKS, CA
U.S.A. 91358**

appreciate any effort you make to speak their language.

Besides the *VOS* form, you will notice that Costa Ricans frequently use many local expressions called **TIQUISMOS**, that are not used in other Latin American countries. Some of the most common expressions are: *PURA VIDA* (fantastic, super, great), *TUANIS* (very good); *BUENA NOTA* (good, OK); *SALADO* (tough luck, too bad); and many others. One saying in particular, *HIJO DE PUTA* (roughly translated as "Son of a B——"), is considered very offensive and vulgar in most Spanish speaking countries, but usually not in Costa Rica if used in the right context. You will be shocked at first when you hear this expressions used so frequently in everyday conversation. Even children and old women can sometimes be heard uttering this phrase. We don't encourage you to use this expression. However, you should be aware that it is a local custom and used most of the time with no malice in mind.

For some basic Spanish phrases and more *tiquismos*, see the section at the end of the book titled "Important Phrases and Vocabulary."

LANGUAGE SCHOOLS

Instituto De La Lengua Española is an excellent intensive program. Six hours daily for 15 weeks - $635. Terms begin in January, May and September. Apdo. 100-2350, San José, Costa Rica. Tel: (506) 227-73-55. Fax: (506) 227-02-11.

Forester Institute International offers a variety of classes plus field trips and the opportunity to live with a family. Prices range from $600 to $1150 depending on the program. Apdo. 6945-1000, San José, Costa Rica. Tel. (506) 225-31-55 Fax: (506) 225-92-36.

INTENSA has two, three and four week programs with home stays available. Prices range from $260 to $545. Apdo. 8110-1000, San José. (506) 225-60-09 Fax: (506) 239-22-25.

Centro Cultural Costarricense Norteamericana has five week courses, three hours daily for $280. Apdo. 1489-1000, San José, Costa Rica.
(506) 225-94-33 Fax: (506) 224-14-80.

Instituto Británico offers a three-week course, three hours a day, with field trips for $1000 including home-stay. Apdo. 8184-1000, San José, Costa Rica. Tel: (506) 234-90-54. Fax: 253-18-94.

Latin America Institute of Language offers various programs including home-stay. Some discounts. Apdo. 1001-2050, San Pedro, San José, Costa Rica. Tel. (506) 225-24-95. Fax: (506) 224-46-65.

Institute for Central American Development Studies offers a one month program, five hours a day, for $892, including classes, lectures, field trips, and home-stay with a Costa Rican family. Apdo. 3-2070 Sabanilla, San José, Costa Rica. Tel: (506) 225-05-08 Fax: (506) 234-13-37.

Academia Costarricense de Lenguaje offers intensive classes and many cultural activities for $975 a month. Apdo. 336-2070, San José, Costa Rica. Tel. (506) 221-16-24 Fax: (506) 233-86-70.

Centro Panamericano de Idiomas is a new school located in a beautiful rural setting. The cost is around $1000 monthly and covers instruction. Home-stay and excursions. Apdo. 947-1000, San José, Costa Rica. Tel: (506) 238-05-61 Fax: (506) 233-86-70.

Mesoamerica Language Institute. Four hours of instruction each day for $80 a week. Apdo. 300-1002, San José, Costa Rica. Tel: (506) 233-77-10.

Academia Tica offers various courses and home-stay that range between $120-$180 for twenty hours of instruction. Apdo. 1294-2100, Guadalupe, San José, Costa Rica. Tel: (506) 234-06-22 Fax: (805) 233-93-93.

DALFA Spanish School offers one month courses for around $1000, including excursions, cultural activities and home-stays. Apdo. 323-1011, San Francisco de Dos Rios. (506) 226-85-84.

Academia Smith Corona offers various courses in downtown San José and Spanish survival courses for tourists. Apdo. 4592-1000, San José, Costa Rica. Tel: (506) 222-46-37.

Centro Lingüístico Latinoamericano offers intensive courses 5 hours per day for four weeks, including home-stay for $900. Apdo. 151, Alajuela, Costa Rica. Tel: (506) 241-02-61.

Centro Lingüístico Conversa offers an excellent conversational program at the main school in San José and another campus located west of town in a rural setting. Prices vary. For more information, write to Apdo. 17-1007, Centro Colón, San José, Costa Rica. Tel: (506) 221-76-49, Fax (506) 233-24-18.

La Escuela D'Amore Spanish Immersion Center. This unique school, located near Costa Rica's beautiful Manuel Antonio Beach on the Pacific Ocean, offers small personal classes with beach lodging or home-stay available. P.O. Box 67, Quepos, Costa Rica. Tel: (506) 710-05-43/U.S.A. (414) 730-3151.

Instituto de Lenguaje "Pura Vida" is located in the beautiful city of Heredia. This school offers a 20% discount to residents of Costa Rica and their families. P.O. Box 730, Garden Grove, CA 92646. Tel: (714) 534-0125. In Costa Rica Tel: (506) 237-03-87.

This list should start you on your way. Private, individualized language classes are also available. Listings can be found in the classified section of the Tico Times newspaper. There is a Spanish conversational club for foreigners who want to improve their Spanish skills-Tel: 254-1433 or 235-7026. The Instituto Universal de Idiomas offers an 'exchange club' where you can practice Spanish with a native speaker in exchange for English (Tel: 257-0441).

COSTA RICA'S INSTITUTIONS OF HIGHER LEARNING

For those of you who wish to continue your education, university level courses are conveniently available to foreigners in subjects such as: business, art, history, political science, biology, psychology, literature, and Spanish, to name a few, as well as all other major academic areas.

Foreigners can enroll directly as special students for their first two years at the University of Costa Rica. Tuition is much lower than most U.S. universities. Students can also audit classes for a nominal fee.

Some of the schools listed below work in conjunction with U. S. universities so that you may earn a degree that is recognized in the United States. You can also study to earn more credits, simply study for fun to increase your general knowledge, or just to stay busy. (See the next chapter for other ways to keep busy.)

- **University of Kansas Office of Studies Abroad**
  204 Lippincott Hall, Lawrence, KS 66045
- **University of California** has a one year program in conjunction with the University of Costa Rica.

- **Associated Colleges of the Midwest**, 18 S. Michigan Ave., Suite 1010, Chicago, IL 60603 has a similar program.
- **National University of San Diego** offers a joint degree program. Apdo. 217-1017 San Jose, C.R. 231-58-55
- **State University of New York** offers enrollment in any discipline to qualified juniors and seniors with two years of Spanish. Conact the office of International Programs L1-84, State University of New York, Albany, NY 12222.

PRIVATE UNIVERSITIES

- **Inter American University of Puerto Rico** phone 225-09-79
- **University for Peace** Apdo. 199-1250, San Jose, C.R. 249-10-72
- **International University of the Americas.** 233-53-04
- **Autonomous University of Central America** - write UACA, Apdo. 7637-1000, San Jose, Costa Rica 441-53-04

PUBLIC UNIVERSITIES

- **University of Costa Rica** - contact Ciudad Universitaria Rodrigo Facio, San Jose, Costa Rica. 224-36-60
- **State University at a Distance** (extension) 225-87-88
- **Univerisad Nacional** 237-66-63
- **Technical Institute of Costa Rica** 551-53-33

Of course, there are certain requirements for the above schools of higher learning. Also, remember that private universities are generally more expensive than public universities.

OUTSTANDING PRIVATE SCHOOLS

Those of you who have small children or teenagers will be pleased to know that Costa Rica has a variety of schools to choose from. There are many public schools, numerous bilingual schools and four English-language, or American Schools.

Costa Ricas private English-language schools are exceptional, have excellent standards and follow the U.S. school year. These private schools are very academically oriented and prepare students for admittance to colleges in the U.S. as well as Costa Rican Universities. In some ways these schools are better than similar institutions in the

U.S.A., in that there seem to be not as many harmful distractions or bad influences in Costa Rica. Your children will also have the opportunity to learn a new language which will be of great value to them later in life. You should be aware of that the cost of some of these private schools can run higher than 200 dollars per month.

Schools that follow the U.S. schedule, September to June:
Costa Rican Academy: Pre-Kindergarden through grade 12. Classes taught in English - U.S. style education. Annual tuition $1,070 for pre-Kindergarden, $3,130 per year for Kindergarden to grade 12. Apdo. 4941-1000, San José, Costa Rica. Tel: (506) 239-03-76.
Country Day School: Kindergarden through grade 12. Located in Escazú. Annual tuition: Pre-Kindergarden $1,245. Grades 1-12, $3,510. Apdo. 8-6170, San José, Costa Rica. Tel: (506) 228-08-73. Fax: (506)228-27-98.
Marian Baker School: Kindergarden - Grade 12. U.S. cirriculum with classes in English. Annual tuition: Kindergarden $2,150; preparatory to grade 6, $2,700; grades 7-8, $2,900; grades 9-12, $3,200. Apdo. 4269, San José, Costa Rica, Tel: (506) 234-46-26 Fax: (506) 234-46-09.
International Christan School: Pre-Kindergarden through grade 12. Annual tuition: Pre-Kingdergarden, $990; Preparatory and Kinder, $1,300; Grades 1-6, $2,200; Grades 7-8, $2,300; Grades 9-12, $2,500. Apdo. 3512-1000, San José, Costa Rica. Tel: 225-14-74.

The less expensive Bilingual private schools below, also prepare students for U.S. Colleges and Universities, but follow the Costa Rican academic year which begins in March and ends in November.
Anglo American School: Kindergarden through grade 6. Costs about $100 a month. Apdo. 3188-1000, San José, Costa Rica. Tel: (506)225-17-29.
Canadian International School: Pre-Kindergarden through grade 2. About $100 monthly. Apdo. 622-2300. San José, Costa Rica. Tel: (506) 224-28-44.
Colegio Humboldt: Kindergarden through grade 12. Classes half in German, half in Spanish. Tuition is around $70 monthly. Apdo. 3749, San José, Costa Rica. Tel: (506) 232-14-55.
Colegio Internacional: Pre-kinder through grade 10. Apdo. 963, 2050 San Pedro, Costa Rica. Tel: (506) 253-12-31 Fax: (506) 253-9762.
Colegio Metodista: Kindergarden through grade 12. Classes in English and Spanish. Apdo. 931-1000, San José, Costa Rica. Tel: (506) 225-06-55.

Escuela Británica: Kindergarden through grade 11, classes half in English, half in Spanish. $150 per month. Apdo. 8184-1000 San José, Costa Rica. Tel: (506) 220-17-19. Fax: (506) 232-78-33.

The European School: Pre-kinder through 6. Apdo. 177, Heredia, Costa Rica. Tel: (506) 237-37-09 Fax: (506) 231-7583.

Liceo Franco-Costarricense: Classes in French, English and Spanish. Concepción de Tres Ríos. Tel: (506) 279-66-16

Lincoln School: Pre-Kindergarden - Grade 12, classes in English. About $100 monthly tuition. Apdo. 1919, San José, Costa Rica. Tel: (506) 235-77-33. Fax: (506) 236-17-06.

Saint Anthony School: Pre-school through grade 6. Classes half in English, half in Spanish. Apdo. 29-2150, Moravia, Costa Rica. Tel: 235-10-17.

Saint Claire: Grades 7-11, classes in English and in Spanish. $125 per month. Apdo. 53-21-50, Moravia, Costa Rica, Tel: (506) 235-72-44.

Saint Francis: Kindergarden - Grade 11, classes in English and Spanish. Inquire about rates. Apdo. 4405-1000, San José Costa Rica. Tel: (506) 235-66-85.

Saint Joseph's Primary School: Pre-school through grade 6, classes half in Spanish, half in English, $70 per month. Apdo. 132-2150, Moravia, Costa Rica. Tel: (506) 235-72-14.

Saint Mary's: Pre- Kindergarden - Grade 6, around $100 monthly, classes in English, and Spanish. Apdo. 229-1250, Escazu, Costa Rica. Tel: (506) 228-20-03.

Santa Monica Primary School: Pre-Kindergarden to grade 6, classes in English and Spanish, around $80 a month. Apdo. 53-2150, Moravia, Costa Rica. Tel: (506) 235-41-19.

Saint Peter's Primary School: Pre-Kindergarden to grade 6, classes in English and Spanish, about $75 monthly. Apdo. 302-2100, Curridabat, Costa Rica. Tel: (506) 253-68-69.

OTHER PRE-SCHOOLS

Centro Educativo Las Vistas. Pre-kinder through grade 3. Apdo 3702, Escazú, Costa Rica. Tel: (506) 228-1763.

Blue Valley School Primary. Apdo. 561, 2050, San Pedro, Costa Rica. Tel. (506) 225-17-29.

El Girasol: Ages 2 and up 232-84-96

Kinder El Conejito: 232-39-53

LaCasa de Los Niños/Montessori: 228-01-68

El Mundo de Peter Pan: 228-49-57

Check the phone book under the section titled **"Escuelas"** for more schools.

CHAPTER FOUR

Keeping Busy

in Costa Rica

SOME SOUND ADVICE

Retirement often presents a new challenge for many people because it is usually the first time in their lives they are confronted with having a lot of leisure time and trying to figure out what to do to stay active. As you will see throughout this chapter, Costa Rica is the perfect place to retire. In addition to being relatively inexpensive there is plenty to do to stay busy and there are many interesting activities to choose from. One retired American stated in reference to his busy life-style in Costa Rica, "My days are so fulfilling, that each day in Costa Rica seems like a whole lifetime."

In Costa Rica you have no excuse for being bored or inactive, unless you are just plain lazy. There is some hobby or pastime for everyone regardless of age or interests. Even if you cannot pursue your favorite hobbies, you should easily be able to get involved in something new and exciting. Best of all, by participating in one or more of the activities we list in this chapter, you will be linked with other people who share common interests and you certainly will cultivate many new friendships in the process. Most of the people you meet will be fellow expatriates, so you probably won't have to know much Spanish to enjoy yourself. You can even spend your time continuing your education or studying Spanish as we talked about in the last chapter.

Whatever you do, don't make the mistake of not staying busy. The worst thing you can do is spend all your time drinking the day away in one of the many *gringo* hangouts in downtown San José. Over the years we have seen many fellow Americans not use their time constructively, and destroy their lives by developing a serious alcohol problem while living in Costa Rica -- a few even died prematurely due to alcohol related circumstances. So, use the information we have provided in this chapter, and take advantage of all that Costa Rica has to offer. Get out and enjoy yourself!

STAY ACTIVE

ENGLISH BOOKS, MAGAZINES AND NEWSPAPERS

Books, newspapers, magazines and other similar printed matter in English are available at most leading bookstores, in the souvenir shops of larger hotels and at some newsstands.

There are many bookstores carrying a very large selection of books in English: **The Bookshop** (Ave 1, Calles 1 and 3) has a good selection and is conveniently located in downtown San José. You can also find English books at **Librería Universal** (Ave. Central, Calles Central and 1), **Librería Lehmann** (Ave. Central, Calles 1 and 3 and Corobicí Hotel).

New books in English are exhorbitantly expensive and sometimes sold at up to three times the U. S. list price. So, you may be better off purchasing your books in the U.S., buying used books or going to a local library.

If you are on a tight budget you can pick up a good used book at **The Book Traders** bookstores located in downtown San José and in the suburb of Escazú. They bill themselves as being the largest used bookstore in Central America. They specialize in selling and trading used books, magazines and compact disks. They also carry guide books, maps and have over 30,000 books in stock. A second store was recently opened in downtown San José on Ave. 1, between Calles 5 & 7, Tel: 255-05-08.

There are also three major libraries in the San José area that have large collections of English language books and magazines.

The place to go for the best selection of books is the **Mark Twain Library** located at the North American - Central American Culture Institute, commonly known as the **Centro Cultural**. You can browse all day or check out books and some magazines. They also have nearly one hundred English magazines to choose from. Call 253-57-83 for more information.

The **National Library**, located near downtown San José, is not a browsing library but has a large selection of novels and magazines in English.

Also, the **University of Costa Rica Library** has some materials in English.

There is no problem obtaining a copy of your favorite *Miami Herald* or *New York Times* newspapers or *Time and Newsweek* magazines in Costa Rica. As we mentioned above, you can pick up most English newspapers and magazines at local newsstands, hotels and some bookstores. You can also arrange to have many of the newspapers we mention in this section delivered to you home or office the same day by calling **Agencia de Publicaciones** at 259-5555, 259-5656, or 259-0812.

OTHER ENGLISH LANGUAGE PUBLICATIONS AVAILABLE:

- *Barron's*
- *International Herald Tribune*
- *Sporting News*
- *Sports Illustrated*
- *USA Today*
- *Wall Street Journal*
- *Washington Post*

The largest newspaper in English published in Central America, *The Tico Times*, is available almost everywhere. Reading it is an excellent way to keep up with local Costa Rican and Central American news in general. Car sales, cultural activities and a lot of other useful information are also found in this newspaper. Even companionship can be found by looking in the personals section of the classified ads. Pick up a copy as soon as you arrive. It comes out every Friday.

To subscribe to the *Tico Times* (if you live in the U.S.) write Dept. 717, P.O. Box 025216, Miami, Florida 33102. If you live in Costa Rica: Apdo.. 4362, San José, Costa Rica.

Another excellent newspaper, **Costa Rica Today,** made its debut recently. This paper is really more for tourists than the *Tico Times* and doesn't carry much news or have much sensationalism like its counterpart. To subscribe write: *Costa Rica Today* 117, P.O. Box 0025216, Miami Fl 33102. There is no need to subscribe locally since you can pick this paper up almost anywhere. It comes out on Thursdays.

TELEVISION AND RADIO

As in the United States, there is satellite cable television in Costa Rica. There are a variety of American television channels for your viewing and entertainment at a low cost from any of the companies listed below. A new cable company, TV America, now offers both the ABC and CBS networks for the first time in Costa Rica. If you don't want to subscribe to cable TV and have a home where you can install your own satellite dish, contact, Orbita, S.A.. Also, there are a limited number of American channels available on UHF for the one time cost of purchasing a UHF antenna.

Most radio stations play Latin music, but some play music in English.

CABLE TELEVISION - To order call the numbers below:

TV AMERICA (CBS & ABC) 226-93-33, 226-90-92

CABLE COLOR .... 231-38-38, 231-28-11 or 231-39-39

SUPER CANAL .... 232-22-44 or 442-19-10

CABLE TICA .... 718-86-14 or 254-88-58

CLUB CABLE .... 551-38-86 or 238-17-56

CHANNEL 19, Master Television

ORBITA, S.A. for satellite dishes .... 223-18-68 Fax 255-06-52

VIDEO RENTALS

Those of you who are video buffs will be happy to know that there are many video rental shops located in the San José area. For a small initial fee you can acquire a membership at one of these stores and enjoy many privileges. Most movies you rent are in English with Spanish subtitles.

Video Flash (Curridabat): 253-73-79
Video de las Américas (two locations): 253-65-45, 257-03-03
Video Express (have delivery and pick up service):... 221-34-66
Video Movies (Curridabat): 253-50-34
Hollywood Video Club (two locations):.. 225-06-30, 227-48-69
Home Movie 2000: 231-43-52
See the phone book for additional listings.

SHOPPING

One way to keep active is to go shopping. Although Costa Rica is not as commericalized as the U.S., you can still spend your free time doing  some serious shopping, browsing or just window shopping.

Because of the large number of U.S. and Canadians living in Costa Rica, and a growing number of Costa Ricans that have been exposed to U.S. culture by watching cable TV and visiting the states, there has been an influx of American products. The only problem is that many of these goods are more expensive in Costa Rica because of import duties.

Everyday there are more and more imported goods from the U.S. available in Costa Rica. Imported brand name cosmetics, stylish clothing, appliances and some foods are a few of the items that can now be found in many stores in San José, and in other areas that cater to foreigners.

There are a number of new stores and shopping centers in or near San José where many of these imported items are now sold. In downtown San José there are specialty shops and a couple of department stores selling American style clothing and other imported goods.

Plaza del Sol, Costa Rica's first U.S.-style mall, is located about five minutes east of San José in the suburb of Curridabat. There is also a small mall located at the the **Auto Mercado Shopping Center** in Rohrmoser.

In the suburb of Escazú, where many foreigners and well-to-do Costa Ricans live, a number of U.S.-style mini-malls have sprung up. Most of these newer stores have the kind of products that foreigners are likely to look for. There is a new, large U.S.-style shopping mall, El Centro Comercial multiplaza to the west of Escazú. When completed this complex will house Costa Rica's largest mall and shopping center.

Despite the availability of many new products, and the growing number of malls, mini-malls and specialty shops, shopping in Costa Rica still leaves a lot to be desired when compared to the U.S. or Canada. You shouldn't expect U.S. style shopping in Costa Rica.

As we mention in Chapter 9, if you plan to live in Costa Rica, you will have to substitute many local products for items you are used to using and do without some of the luxuries and goods found in the U.S. This is easy to do since there is a variety of similar products available in Costa Rica. However, if you must have products from the states, you can routinely make trips to the U.S. every few months as many foreigners and wealthy Costa Ricans do, to stock up on such, items as canned goods and other non-perishable foods, clothing, sundries and cosmetics. We know of one American retiree who goes to Miami every three of four months to buy all the products and goodies he can't find in Costa Rica. These frequent trips to the states are really unecessary if you don't want to spend money on airplane tickets and can learn to make do with the local products.

COSTA RICAN PASTIMES

Costa Rica has a wealth of activities both indoors or outdoors, designed with everybody in mind regardless of sex, age, personal taste or budget. Costa Ricans as well as tourists and foreign residents can enjoy the following activities: river rafting (some of the world's best), bird watching, camping, ceramics classes, dance, racquetball, rollerskating, volleyball, weight lifting, walking groups, tennis, baseball, basketball, soccer, surfing, wind surfing, bowling, hiking, football, running, bicycling, flying, horseback riding, hang gliding, sailing, jet skiing and sun bathing as well as opera, plays, movies, bridge, art galleries, social clubs, libraries, museums, parks, zoos and many other activities.

Check the activities section of the *Tico Times*, or *Costa Rica Today*.
For those of you who wish to join a private athletic club, country
club or gym we suggest the following:

The Indoor Club in Curridabat:..................................... 225-93-44
The Spa Corobicí:... 232-81-22
Costa Rican Tennis Club:... 232-12-66
Costa Rican Country Club in Escazú:....................... 228-93-33
Cariari Country Club (golf):.. 239-24-55
Bello Horizonte Country Club:.................................. 228-09-24
Costa Rica Yacht Club:... 223-42-24
Spa Cariari Hotel:... 239-00-22
Club Olímpico:.. 228-50-51

Look under gyms (gimnásios) in the yellow pages for more
listings.

FISHING IN COSTA RICA

For those who like to spend leisure time fishing, Costa Rica is the
perfect place to retire. Costa Rica has some of the best sportfishing in
the world and a large variety of fish. Take your choice. Fish either the
Caribbean or the Pacific, but don't forget those gentle miles of
meandering rivers and fresh water lakes. Lake Arenal is famous for
its great fishing and *guapote* trout. More important, on any given day,
most of these fishing areas are only a few hours driving time from
where you are in Costa Rica.

Costa Rica is considered by many to be one of the best year-round
fishing areas in the world. The fishing is outstanding almost all of the
time and almost everywhere in Costa Rica, except when it rains now
and then-but even then it really isn't so bad since your chance of
hooking some excellent sport fish are very good. When it comes to
sailfish, tarpon or snook, no place is better.

If you are really "hooked" on fishing, and want to keep up with
the local fishing scene, we suggest you pick up a copy of the *Tico Times*
or *Costa Rica Today* newspapers. Both papers have excellent weekly
fishing columns. The column in *Costa Rica Today* is written by the
legendary fishing columnist Jerry Ruhlow who is rumored to be
presently working on a book about fishing in Costa Rica.

If you want the most up-to-date fishing information, we suggest
you contact **American Fishing Services**. Tell them what type of fish

you want to catch and they will help you. Their office is conveniently located in the Hotel Del Rey in downtown San José, one block south of Morazan Park. For more information call or fax and ask to speak to Richard Krug, the local fishing expert, at Tel: 011-506-221-72-72 or Fax: 011-506-221-00-96.

First look at some of the fishing camps on the Caribbean Coast that have great accommodations and experienced English-speaking fishing guides.

Carribbean Fishing:
Tortuga Lodge: 223-03-33
Parismina Tarpon Rancho:.. 235-77-66
Casamar:.. 441-28-20
Río Colorado: .... 232-40-63 or 232-86-10
Isla de Pesca: .... 221-53-96 or 223-19-73

Pacific Fishing:
Flamingo Bay Pacific Charters:.................. 680-04-44 or 680-06-20
Bahía Pez Vela: (Ocotal) .... 221-15-86 or 670-01-29
Papagayo Excursions: 680-08-59
Oasis del Pacífico: (Nicoya) 661-15-55
Sports Fishing Quepos:... 233-91-35
Costa Rican Dreams: (Quepos) 777-05-93
Tango Mar: (Tambor) 661-27-98
Hotel Flor de Itabo: (Playas del Coco) 670-02-92
Golfito Sports Fishing: 775-03-53
Reel'n Release Sportfishing: (Dominical)........................ 771-19-03
Blue Marlin Fishing: (Flamingo Beach) 654-40-43

Freshwater Trout Fishing:
Adventuras Tilarán: (Arenal)... 695-50-08
Finca Zacatecales:.. 771-17-32

Nearly all of these fishing camps and lodges have overnight accommodations available including meals. Fishing equipment and boats are also provided.

For the listing of other fishing camps and tours, read the *Tico Times* and *Costa Rica Today* or consult a local travel agency.

COSTA RICA'S PRISTINE BEACHES

Unlike many resort areas in Mexico and Latin America, Costa Rica's beautiful tropical beaches and 767 miles of coastline are virtually unspoiled. Water temperatures are very warm so you can stay in all day.

Moving from north to south along the west coast you will find many white sand and dark sand beaches and resorts.

In the Guanacaste there are the following beaches: Playa Naranjo, Playa Panama, Playa Hermosa, Play del Coco (a favorite gringo hangout) Ocotal, Bahía Pez Vela, Playa Protrero, Playa Flamingo, Playa Brasilito, Conchal, Playa Grande, Playa Tamarindo, Playa Avellana, and Playa Junquillal.

As we move south the following beaches are located along the Nicoya Peninsula: Playa Azul, Playa Nosara, Playa Samara, Playa Carrillo, Playa Coyote. Playas Naranjo and Montezuma on the eastern tip of Nicoya, are both nice beaches.

Moving even farther south along the Pacific Coast are: Puntarenas - Costa Rica's main port, Boca Barranca - good surfing beach, Mata Limón, Playa Tivives, Playa Tarcoles, Playa Escondido, Playa Herradura, Playa Jacó, Playa Hermosa, Esterillos, Quepos, Manuel Antonio (considered by many to be the most beautiful beach in Costa Rica) and Playa Dominical.

On the Atlantic side are: Playa Bonita (portete), Punta Cahuita (beautiful beach), Puerto Viejo, Playa Uva and Playa Manzanillo.

NATIONAL PARKS FOR NATURE LOVERS

Costa Ricans take pride in their extensive national park system. Since Costa Rica is not only rich in natural beauty but all types of wild life, Costa Ricans have set aside 20 % of their territory and established 36 national parks and preserves to protect the flora and fauna of their country.

Costa Rica's parks are located in every region of the country with some being more easily reached than others. The variety of birds, butterflies, amphibians, mammals, trees and flowers has to be seen to be believed.

Additional information and a list of parks may be obtained by calling 233-56-73, 233-52-84 or 233-41-60. Most hotels and tourist information centers can be helpful to nature lovers. Please note since reserves are more strictly protected than parks a permit is usually necessary.

MAKING NEW FRIENDS IN COSTA RICA

You should have no problem making new friends in Costa Rica, but might have some difficulty meeting Costa Ricans if you speak little or no Spanish. Nevertheless, you will be surprised how many Costa Ricans speak some English and like yourself are dying for the chance to perfect their English language skills while you work on your Spanish. Perhaps you can find someone to exchange language lessons with. This is a good way to make new acquaintances and learn how Spanish is really spoken.

You most certainly will find it easier to meet fellow Americans in Costa Rica than in the U.S., because for some reason Americans living abroad tend to gravitate toward each other. Newcomers only have to find an enclave of fellow countrymen and they can make many new friends. You can't help bumping into other Americans since Costa Rica is such a small country (there are over 20,000 gringos living there permanently). This is especially true if you live in one of the areas or neighborhoods where many North Americans reside, like Escazú or Rohrmoser. Another good way of making contact with other expatriats is by participating in some of the activities listed in the weekly editions of the local English newspapers, *Tico Times* and *Costa Rica Today*. These newspapers serve as a vital link in the foreign community, or "Gringo Grapevine", as we call it, and help to put you in contact with the whole network of expatriates and the services they offer.

By occasionally frequenting any of the local gringo "watering holes" in downtown San José, like Nashville South, Tiny's Tropical Sports Bar or the Piano Blanco Bar, you can watch live sporting events from the U.S. on cable T.V. or simply shoot the breeze with your fellow compatriots. Many Americans also hang out downtown around the Plaza de La Cultura and at the McDonald's across the street, where they may be seen sipping coffee every morning and watching the many beautiful women pass by. You have no reason to be lonely unless you just want to be. Just be yourself and you will find Costa Rica is just the place for you. Oh yes, we might add that there are poetry readings, art and sculpture exhibitions as well as many of the other activities we have listed under Costa Rican pastimes in this chapter where people easily socialize. The American Costa Rican Cultural Center has many events where you certainly can make new acquaintances.

CLUBS:
American Legion Post 10 (Escazú): 228-17-40
Asociación de Pensionados Rentistas (provides help and
   advice to foreign retirees and investors):......................223-17-33
Women's Club of Costa Rica: 222-18-15

* For a complete listing of clubs and related activities, look under the weekly "What's Doing" section in the *Tico Times*, or in the Calendar of Events section in the newspaper, *Costa Rica Today*.

FINDING LOVE AND PERMANENT COMPANIONSHIP

If you are looking for someone of the opposite sex for romance, Costa Rica might just be the right place for you.

Ladies, regardless of age you will have plenty of gentleman admirers if you so desire. Due to *machismo* Costa Rican men tend to be more flirtatious and aggressive than North American men. Most Costa Rican men perceive foreign women to have looser morals and to be easier "conquests" than *ticas* (Costa Rican women.) So, be careful to take time to develop a long-term, meaningful relationship and don't rush things.

Men of all ages, no matter how they may view themselves in their own culture or other cultures, will have no problem meeting Costa Rican women. Costa Rican women have an unparalleled reputation as being the most uniformly BEAUTIFUL, FLIRTATIOUS, and ACCESSIBLE women in Latin America -- including Brazil. The ladies of Costa Rica consider you a joy and are more warm-hearted and eternally devoted than their North American counterparts. A man doesn't even have to be rich to meet women — an $800 Social Security check translates to a millionaire's pay in Costa Rica. It is no wonder that Costa Rican women are highly sought by foreign men. However, before becoming involved with a Costa Rican woman, you should realize that there are many cultural differences that can lead to all sorts of problems later on, especially if you don't speak Spanish fluently.

Generally, Latin women are more jealous and possessive than American women, and tend not to understand our ways unless they have had the chance to live in the United States. Also, be aware that because of their comparative wealth, most Americans, especially the elderly, are considered prime targets for some unscrupulous Latin females.

As we alluded to at the end of the first chapter, in some cases there is another bad side of marrying a Costa Rican woman in that you can end up supporting her whole family either directly or indirectly as many foreigners complain. There is a book titled, "Happy Aging With Costa Rican Women - The Other Costa Rica" by James Y. Kennedy (published by Box Canyon Books). This book tells all about the trials and tribulations and experiences of many *gringos* with Costa Rican women.

We advise you to give any relationship time and make sure a woman is sincerely interested in you and not just your money — you will be saving yourself a lot of grief and heartache in the long run. Since prostitution is legal and accessible to men of all ages, be careful of these ladies of "ill-repute." Many foreigners have invited one of these females to spend the night with them, only to wake up the next day without the woman and minus their wallets and other valuables.

Most single men can avoid getting involved with gold diggers, prostitutes, or other troublesome women if they know where to look for good women. The personals section of the *Tico Times* is an excellent place to advertise for companionship. It is relatively inexpensive and many Costa Rican women read this section each week. Many foreigners have found their wives this way. Check out the current or past issues of the *Tico Times* for ideas as to how to write one of these ads. One American we know ran an ad and screened hundreds of women before finding his ideal mate. As far as we know to this day he is still happily married. Taking classes at the universities is another way to meet quality women. Finally, if you have Costa Rican friends, they will usually introduce you to someone who is worthwhile.

NIGHTLIFE AND ENTERTAINMENT

There are countless open air restaurants, bars, dance halls and discotheques all over San José and in most other parts of the country. Costa Ricans love to party and dance. No doubt once you have lived in the country for a while, you will be bitten by the dance bug. If you want to learn to dance like a Latin, you can call 221-16-24 or 233-89-14 for lessons.

San José's many discotheques and dance halls play a variety of music for all tastes until the wee hours of the morning and admission is inexpensive or free. International liquors and cocktails are served, as well as all local beers and beverages. Also, keep in mind that many of these clubs serve food and their traditional heaping plates of delicious local appetizers or hôrs d'oeuvres, called *Bocas*.

Most of these establishments are quiet by day and artistically decorated. Many have adjoining restaurants, live music or a disc jockey, and well-lighted dance floors.

For those of you who want something more romantic and quiet, let's not forget the famous mariachis at La Esmeralda who will serenade you with their guitars, trumpets and violins all through the night.

WHERE TO GO FOR NIGHTLIFE - ENTERTAINMENT

Amstel Hotel Lounge... Simple, elegant, quiet.
Antojitos... Good Mexican food.
Bar Mexico... Live music.
Chelles... People watching hangout.
Chelles Taberna... Another people watching hangout.
Classic Rock & Roll Bar... Good Rock.
Cocoloco... Large disco located at El Pueblo Shopping Center.
Dennies... Quiet bar & restaurant, live music.
El Cuartel de La Boca del Monte... Good Place.
Infinito... Another disco found at El Pueblo Shopping Center.

La Esmeralda… Lots of fun here, live music.
Mirador Ram Luna… Family style, jukebox, dancing.
Rokola's... Favorite tunes from the 60's and 70's.
Soda La Perla... Meeting place.
Salsa 54... Great dancing downtown.
Tunel del Tiempo... More dancing downtown.
La Plaza... Elegant with large dance floor.
Cocodrilo... Located in San Pedro, fun.
Baleares... Also in San Pedro, good live Latin Jazz music.
El Gran Parqueo...Good Latin dancing.
Los Higuerones… Latin Dancing in a large dance hall.
Los Tunas...Restaurant, bar, discotheque.
Bar Atlas...Discotheque, happy hour.
Bromelia's Cafe and Grill...Live cool jazz and happy hour.
Friday's...Located in San Pedro, great American style food, drink
and atmosphere.

THE GRINGO BAR SCENE

As we wrote about earlier there are a number of *gringo* bars, which cater almost exclusively to expatriates, located in downtown San José or nearby. Although we don't recommend hanging out at these places 24-hours a day, there is no better way to hear stories about life in the tropics, keep up on local gossip, meet some colorful local characters and learn many tips about living in Costa Rica while you sip your favorite beverage.

One of our favorite watering holes is **Tiny's Tropical Sports Bar**. It is considered San José's best sports bar and packed during any major sporting event. You should check out their annual Super Bowl and Saint Patrick's day parties. They have large color televisions for such occasions.

Lucky's Piano Bar located next door to the hotel Balmoral, is a people watching bar because of its large plate glass window that provides a view of busy Avenida Central.

Nashville South is a country western bar with an interesting clientele and western decor.

Another *gringo* hangout is the bar at the **Dunn Inn Hotel**. You can meet plenty of expatriates here. The owner, Pat "Tex" Dunn used to run Nashville South and a couple of other gringo bars. He is a congenial man who can provide you with a lot of information about living in Costa Rica.

Five minutes from downtown, in the suburb of Los Yoses, you will find one of the area's hottest new bars- **Catástrofe** (Catastrophe). This bar used to be run by a long-time Costa Rican character and legend, the late Jimmy Adams. Another great *gringo* bar is the ***Blue Marlin Bar*** located in the Hotel Del Rey. This bar is frequented by many sport enthusiasts. You are likely to hear a lot of friendly boasting and some tall fish tales at this unique bar. If you're looking to make some acquaintances, this bar is worth visiting.

The dingy **New York Bar**, **Happy Days** and **The Park Hotel Bar**, are other bars in downtown San José where you can find Americans and Canadians, some locals and many "Ladies of the night". Speaking of night clubs, the **Key Largo**, located across from Morazán Park in a beautiful, old mansion is where you can hear live music nightly and find female companionship, if you so desire. This bar generally fills up around 10:00 p.m.

The **American Bar**, located in Escazú is another bar where many *gringos* hangout.

FULL SERVICE COCKTAIL BARS

Most bars open at 11 a.m. and close at 2 a.m....7 days per week. Some have happy hours.

Risas... Nice quaint atmosphere. Home of the Costa Rican yuppie set. The owners are from the U.S.

Promesas... Avenida Central. Good for people watching.

Charleston... Nice ambience.

Las Yuntas... Great snacks with each drink.

Hotel Corobicí... Good bar.

Holiday Inn... Across from Morazán Park.

Hotel Izazú... Two drinks for one on Fridays.

Nashville South... Warm friendship for everyone.

La Soda Tapia... Nice place to drink across from the Sabana Park.

Hotel Balmoral... Nice quiet bar.

Shakespeare Bar... Cocktails, piano and darts.

Yesterday's... Downtown San José.

Soda Palace... Open 24 hours, across from Central Park.

Besito's Bar... Good music on tape and TV.

Marley's... Ave 1--downtown.

Taberna Cayuco-Calle 11, Ave 1& 3, X-rated movies.

TX... In San Pedro, good drinks.

Bar EL Higueron... Also in San Pedro.

Josephine's... Live dance shows and good nightclub.

GAMBLING

Costa Rica has around twenty casinos with most in the San José area and a few located at various beach resorts. Rules are slightly different here than in the U.S.A. or Europe, but gambling is fun to learn the COSTA RICAN way. There are four legal casino games. Rummy, a variation of black jack or 21, is the most popular of these casino games. Craps, roulette (played lottery style rather than with a wheel) and *tute* a type of poker played against the house. Slot machines and sports betting are illegal and not permitted. Most casinos give away free drinks while you play and are opened from around 6 p.m. to 3 or 4 a.m. The Grand Hotel Costa Rica has 24-hour gambling.

WHERE TO GO:
- San José Palacio (The newest, largest and best casino in the country)
- Hotel Cariari
- Holiday Inn (Check out the panoramic wiew of San José)
- Balmoral Hotel
- Hotel Corobicí
- Hotel Irazú
- Hotel Presidente
- Club Triángulo
- Hotel Sheraton Herradura
- Hotel Costa Rica
- Le Chambord Restaurant
- Royal Garden
- Club colonial

The most popular form of gambling in Costa Rica is the national lottery or *lotería*. This game of chance is played a couple of times each week. You can purchase a whole sheet of tickets or a fraction of a ticket from any street venor. A substantial amount of money may be won if you have a winning ticket. If you are lucky enough to win the huge, annual Christmas Lottery, or *Gordo Navideño* as it is called, you will become very rich and probably set for life. To find out the results of the lottery, look in the local newspaper.

There is also an instant winner type of lottery similar to what is played in the U.S., called *raspa*. In this game you scrape off the covering of the ticket with a coin to see if you have the matching symbols or numbers.

MOVIES AND THEATERS

There are movie theaters conveniently located all over the San José area and in other large cities. Most of these theaters show first-run movies usually about a month or two after they first screen in the United States. About 40% of all current hit movies shown in the United States make their way to Costa Rica sooner or later. You shouldn't worry about understanding these movies since they are all in English with Spanish subtitles. You can read the local newspapers to see what movies are currently playing. At present, admission is a little over two dollars.

San José is purported to have more theatres and theatre companies per capita than any other city in the world. Most live plays are in Spanish but there are occasional plays in English at the North American Cultural Center. However, by going to plays presented in Spanish, you can improve your language skills. Current stage plays are also listed in the activities section of local newspapers.

MOVIES (CINES)

Cine Bellavista: 221-09-09
    Ave. Central, Calles 17 & 19
Cine California: 221-47-38
    Calle 23, Ave. 1
Cine Capri: 223-02-64
    Ave. Central, Calles 9 & 1
Cine Magaly: 223-00-85
    Calle 23, Ave. Central & 1
Cine Omni: 221-79-03
    Behind Macdonald's and the Plaza de la Cultura
Cine Rex: 221-00-41
    Calle Central, Avenida 6 & 8
Cine Universal: 221-52-41
    Paseo Colón, Calle 26 & 28

Cine Colón: 221-45-17
    Centro Colón Building
Sala Garbo: 222-10-34
    100 Meters south of Pizza Hut Paseo Colón
Cine Variedades 222-61-04
    Ave. Central & 1 Calle 5

THEATERS *(TEATROS)* IN AND AROUND

Teatro La Comedia 255-32-55
    Next to Más por Menos Market on Ave. Central
Teatro Laurence Olivier 222-10-34
    Ave. 2, Calle 28
Teatro Arlequin 222-07-92
    Calle 13, Ave. Central
Sala J.J. Vargas Calvo 222-18-75
    Calles 3 & 5, Ave. 2
Teatro del Angel 222-82-58
    Ave. Central & Plaza de la Democracia
Teatro Melico Salazar 221-49-52
    Ave. 2, Calle Central
Teatro de La Aduana 223-45-63
    Calle 25, Avenidas 3 & 5
Teatro Capra 234-28-66
    Calles 29 & 33, Ave. 1
Teatro Chaplin 223-29-19
    Paseo de Los Estudiantes
Teatro Calle 15 222-66-26
    Calle 15, Avenida 2
Teatro Máscara 255-42-50
    Calle 13, Avenidas 2 & 4
Facultad de Bellas Arles
    University of Costa Rica

CHAPTER FIVE

Getting Around

AIR TRAVEL TO, IN AND AROUND COSTA RICA

Most direct flights cost less through Miami, however there are flights from your home city to San José via Los Angeles, Houston, New Orleans, or Panama. The following airlines offer service from the United States to San José, Costa Rica: AVIATECA, SASHA, CONTINENTAL, MEXICANA, TACA, AMERICAN, UNITED, AERO COSTA RICA (1-800-237-6274) and LACSA - Costa Rica's national airline. You may contact Lacsa toll-free by calling 1-800-255-2272 in the U.S.A. and 1-800-663-2444 in Canada.

Some airline tickets are good for a year, but you have to get permission from the Costa Rican Immigration Department to stay in the country for longer than 90 days, unless you have Costa Rican residency or are a *pensionado*. Most airlines offer special excursion rates and 3 or 4 week packages. Others, especially Canadian airlines, offer special group and charter rates. Fares are subject to availability and change and/or restrictions which may include advanced purchase requirements, minimum stops and cancellation penalties. Remember the main tourist season in Costa Rica runs from about Thanksgiving to Easter. This period approximately coincides with local vacations as well, so it is hard to find available space at this time of

LACSA -
COSTA RICA'S AIRLINE

year. If you are planning to travel to or from Costa Rica during December you may have to buy a ticket months in advance because of the Christmas holidays. However, if you get into a jam you can sometimes find space on a flight via Panama.

Finally, if you plan to travel or explore South America from your home in Costa Rica, in most cases, you can save money by flying first to Miami and then buying a round trip ticket to your destination. For instance, a one-way ticket from San José to Buenos Aires, Argentina alone can end up costing more than a round trip ticket from Miami to Buenos Aires. So, check out prices via Miami to other Latin American destinations.

INTERNATIONAL AIRLINES LOCATED IN SAN JOSE, COSTA RICA

Aero Peru, Ave 5 Calle 1: 441-09-44
Areolíneas Argentinas, Ave 1 Calle 3-5: 222-13-32
Air France, Ave 1 Calle 4-6: 222-88-11
Alitalia, Ave ct. 1 Calle 1-3: 222-61-38
American Airlines, La Sabana: 222-56-55
Avianca/SAM, Ave 5 Calle 1: 221-33-11
British Airways, Ave 5 Calle 1: 223-56-48
Continental, Juan Santamaria Airport: 233-02-66
COPA, Ave 5 Calle 1: 222-70-33
Iberia, Ave 2-4 Calle 1: 221-33-11
KLM 220-41-41
Korean Air, Ave 1 Calle 3-5: 222-47-37
LACSA, La Uruca: 231-00-33
Lan Chile, Lobby Hotel Torremolinos: 222-17-11
Mexicana 222-17-11
Nica 222-17-44
Sasha, Ave 5 Calle 1-3: 221-57-74
TACA 222-17-10
United 220-48-44

DOMESTIC AIRLINES

Smaller domestic airlines like SANSA or special charters, called air taxis, are used for flights within the country. The latter are very expensive, costing up to a few hundred dollars an hour. SANSA, the national airline, is more reasonalbly priced ($15 to $30, depending on your destination). SANSA flies to the beach cities of Golfito,

Quepos, Barra del Colorado, Samara, Nosara, and Tamarindo. It is recommended that you purchase your tickets in advance, especially during the heavy tourist season (December to May.) These flights are the fastest way to get to your designation for your money, save you time and give you the thrill of viewing Costa Rica's spectacular landscape from above.

The SANSA office is located at Paseo Colón and Calle 24. Telephone 33-53-30 for flight times and reservations. Reservations can also be made at some travel agencies in San José.

AIR TAXIS

AVIONES TAXI AEREO S.A. .... 441-16-26 OR 441-20-62
TAXI AEREO CENTRO AMERICANO S.A. 232-13-17 or 232-14-38
TRAVELAIR .... 332-78-83 or 320-30-54
or look in the yellow pages under "Taxis Aereos."

TRAVELING BY BUS IN COSTA RICA

As you already know, bus fares within San José and surrounding suburbs are very affordable. Also, for a very low cost ($2 - $6, or about $1 per hour of driving time) you can find a bus going almost anywhere in the country. Since many Costa Ricans don't own cars, they depend on this form of transportation for traveling to other parts of the country. Traveling by bus provides the perfect opportunity to get to know the people on a personal basis, see the lovely countryside and to learn something about the country and the culture. Most of the buses used for these longer trips are modern vehicles, and very comfortable. Unlike some parts of Latin America, Costa Rica's buses are not filled with chickens and other small animals and NO standing is allowed. Buses can be rather crowded on weekends and holidays. so try to buy your tickets in advance or get to the station early. Be sure to check for schedule changes.

Alajuela (a bus every 20 minutes or so) Ave 2,
    Streets 12 & 14 222-53-25
Cañas (get tickets in advance) Street 16, Ave 1-3 222-30-06
Cartago (a bus every 10 minutes) Street 13,
    Central Avenue-2 233-53-50
Golfito (get tickets in advance) Streets 2-4 221-42-14
Heredia (a bus every 5 minutes) Street 1, Ave 7-9 233-83-92
Liberia (get tickets in advance) Street 14, Ave 1-3 222-16-50

Limón (a bus every hour, 6 am to 6 pm, get tickets in advance on
holidays) Ave 3, Street 19-21 223-78-11
Nicoya (get tickets in advance) Ave 3-5 222-27-50
Ojo de Agua (a bus every 30 minutes) Ave 1, Street 18-20
Puntarenas (a bus every 30 minutes, get to the station
early on holidays) Street 12, Ave 7-9 222-00-64
Quepos (get tickets in advance inside the market)
Coca Cola Terminal 223-55-67
San Carlos (a bus every hour) Coca Cola Terminal 255-43-18
Santa Cruz (get tickets in advance) Street 14, Ave 1-3 221-72-02
San Isidro del General (get tickets in advance)
Street 16, Ave 1-3 .... 223-35-77, 223-06-81, 222-24-22
Sarchí (ride the NARANJO BUS, every hour)
Street 16, Ave 1-3 441-37-81
Southern Border (Paso Canoas, leaves daily)
Ave 18, Streets 2-4 223-76-85
Tilarán - (leaves daily) Street 14, Ave 9-11 222-38-54
Turrialba Calle 13, Ave 6-8 556-00-73
Zona Sur (get tickets in advance) Ave 18, Street 4 221-42-14

* If your destination is not listed on this page, you should check with
a local travel agency, the tourist office located under the Plaza de La
Cultura in downtown San José, or try to find some knowledgable
person who is familiar with bus schedules and knows where different
buses leave from.

BUS TRAVEL TO AND FROM COSTA RICA

If you ever want to travel to Guatemala, Panama or any other
Central American country, you can use the bus services we list here.
Also, if you want to live in Costa Rica permanently without becoming
a legal resident you can take one of these buses to Panama or Nicaragua,
return to Costa Rica 72 hours later, and thus renew your papers so that
you can legally stay in the country for another 90 days. Many
foreigners, who live as perpetual tourists in Costa Rica, go through
this procedure every few months in order to avoid immigration
hassles. Note: This is illegal and we do **not** recommend it.

From time to time the immigration department has been known
to ask for proof of a return ticket as a requirement for extending
tourist cards. In this case it is a good idea to buy an inexpensive bus

ticket to a neighboring country to prove that you have the means to leave the country at any given time.

San José to Panama City leaves daily at 10 p.m. from Avenida 4 between Calles 9 and 11. The 542 mile journey takes twenty hours. Tel: (221-89-54).

San José to David (Panama) leaves daily at 7:30 a.m. from Avenida 18 between Calles 2 and 4. Makes the 240 mile trip in 9 hours. Tel: (221-42-14).

San José to Managua, Nicaragua leaves at 7 a.m. The 270 mile trip takes about 11 hours. Tel: (221-89-54) (223-14-64).

San José to Guatemala leaves daily at 7:30 a.m. from Avenida 4 between Calles 9 and 11. This trip takes 2-1/2 days. Tel: (221-89-54).

TRAVELING BY TRAIN

Unfortunately, train service on Costa Rica's two main rail lines has been discontinued. The famous "Jungle Train" that ran from San José to the Caribbean port of Limón met its demise because of landslides caused by an earthquake. Despite being a slow mode of transportation and more suited for tourists, this train ride was known for its breathtaking scenery. Hopefully someday this rail line will be open again.

Train service was also halted between San José and the Pacific port of Puntarenas. At present there is some talk of resuming this service sometime in the future.

Currently, there are only a few types of train service available in Costa Rica. There is a commuter train that runs from the University of Costa Rica, in the suburb of San Pedro, to the town of Heredia. This train leaves Heredia at 6:15 a.m., 1 p.m., and 6 p.m. and returns from San Pedro at 12 noon and 5 p.m. The trip takes around 45 minutes.

San Jose's inner-city train service, Intertren, runs from the Pacific Railway Station (Avenida 20, Calle 2) to the suburb of Pavas. Trains leave from San José at 6 a.m., 12:15 p.m. and 5:15 p.m. and costs about 20 colons (15 cents).

OLD LIMON JUNGLE TRAIN

Intertren expanded its current service from San José to the city of Cartago, about 20 kilometers east in October 1993.

* NOTE: At times train service throughout the country is subject to suspension.

TAXIS AND AUTOMOBILE RENTALS

As we mentioned in Chapter 2, it is not necessary to own an automobile if you live in San José or nearby because taxis are both plentiful and inexpensive. San Jose´s buses are cheaper but taxis are the best way to get from point A to point B.

Taxis charge 80 colones for the first kilometer and 30 colones per kilometer thereafter. They can be rented by the hour for 600 to 1000 colones. There is also a charge for stopping time equivalent to charge for one kilometer on the meter. Also, if you take a taxi between 10 p.m. and 5 a.m. the driver can charge you 20% above the meter fare. If you want the driver to wait for you while you do an errand or some other business, the official rate is 300 colones an hour. If you have to go more than 12 kilometers outside of the metropolitan area, there is another rate.

Nearly all taxis have computerized meters called *Marías*. Always insist that your taxi driver use his meter and be sure to ask about rates before traveling anywhere.

If you are overcharged or dissatisfied with service you can take the taxi driver's permit number, usually located on the visor of his cab, or his license number and complain to the MOPT Office *Ministerio de Obras Públicas y Transporte* located at Plaza Víquez. You can do this in person, by letter or over the telephone.

Most taxi drivers know how to get to those hard to find, out of the way places and how to locate those almost non-existent addresses around San José. Most houses don't have a numbering system or address. You should have no problem getting a taxi since there are around 2,500 taxis in the San José area. They can be found around every public square and park, parked outside discoteques, on most busy streets and in front of government buldings and most hotels. Be careful since many taxis that park in front of hotels try to charge more.

You should be aware that it is difficult to find a cab during the rainy season, especially in the afternoon when it generally rains the most. You may also have trouble getting a cab weekdays during rush hour between 7 a.m. and 9 a.m. and 4:30 p.m. to 6:30 p.m.. To hail a cab just yell, "Taxi!" If a cab is parked just say the word "Libre" (available) to the driver. If the cab is available he will usually nod his head or say, "sí" (yes).

If you want to stay on a cab drivers good side, never slam the taxis doors. Cabs are expensive in Costa Rica and cab drivers try to maintain their cabs in as good shape as possible.

There are some people who moonlight or work as taxi drivers using their own unmarked cars. They are called *piratas* (pirates) by the locals, and will often approach you if they see you are looking for a cab. Since they don't have meters we advise you not to use any of these vehicles for transportation.

If you ever need to call a cab you should be able to give your exact location in Spanish, this way the taxi driver will know where to pick you up. You should know that if you call a cab by phone, the driver is allowed to turn on the meter where he got the call and charge for the driving time to get to your location. Airport pick-ups can be reserved in advance by calling one of the cab companies.

You can find the telephone numbers of the local cab companies in the yellow pages of the telephone book under the heading "Taxi." The *Copeguari* and *Copetico* taxi companies have the largest number of available cabs 24-hours a day. Many of these companies also rent big trucks, or *Taxis de Carga*, at a very low hourly rate. These vehicles can be very helpful if you ever have to move furniture to or from your house or apartment.

If you ever need to rent a car there are major international car rental agencies and private car rentals conveniently located all over San José. Most rental agencies operate like those in the United States. The cost of renting a vehicle will depend on the year, model and make of car. You must be at least 18 years old and have any valid driver's license, have either an American Express, Visa or Master Card or be able to leave a large deposit. Also, remember insurance is extra. Always phone or make arrangements for car rentals well in advance.

AVIS - Sabana norte 232-99-22
BUDGET - Calle 30, Paseo Colón 223-32-84
DOLLAR - Calle Central, Ave 9 233-33-39
NATIONAL - Calle Central, Ave 9 233-33-39
SANTOS - Located at the Airport 441-30-44

For other car rental agencies see the yellow pages or the *Tico Times* newspaper for ads.

Also, in the *Tico Times* there are ads for private drivers or chauffers. This is a good alternative to taxis but can be rather expensive.

DRIVING IN COSTA RICA

You may drive in Costa Rica just as in the United States when you have a Costa Rican driver's license, which is required if you are a resident or *pensionado*. If you are a tourist you can use your U.S. license.

It is really easy to obtain a Costa Rican driver's license. First, you have to go to the office where driver's licenses are issued, located one block west of Plaza Víquez on the southwest corner. Then if you already have a license from your own country, it's only a matter of transferring information, taking some photos, paying a small processing fee, taking an eye-exam, having a little patience and you will have your license in a matter of hours. If you do not have a current driver's license you will have to take a driver's test just as in the states, but it's all worthwhile.

Whether you are renting a car or using your own automobile it is important to make sure you always keep the right kind of documents in your car. We suggest you check with your lawyer to see what documents are required. Also, if you are a *pensionado* and your car has special *pensionado* plates the police will occasionally stop you to see if all of your paperwork is in order. If a policeman should stop you, above all be polite, stay calm, and do not be verbally abusive. Most traffic police are courteous and helpful. However, if you commit a traffic violation some policemen will try to have you pay for your ticket on the spot. Be advised this is not the standard procedure. If this does happen to you there are two offices where you can complain. You can file your complaints with the Judicial Police (O.I.J.) or with the Legal Department of the Transit Police (tel: 227-21-88). Finally, if you are involved in a traffic accident, **don't move your car** and be sure to contact the local traffic police (Tel. 222-71-50, 227-80-30) so that they can make out a report.

Be very careful when driving in San José or any other large city. Most streets in San José are narrow, one-way and very crowded due to heavy traffic. Also, the names of the streets are not located on sign posts on the street corners as in the United States. Most streets' names are found on small blue signs attached to the sides of buildings. Some streets don't even have signs. When driving in the countryside, only drive during the day, watch out for livestock, and be sure to use some kind of map. Don't get off the main paved road unless absolutely necessary during the rainy season if your car does not have four-wheel drive. You may end up getting stuck in the mud. Unfortunately, the only way to get to some of Costa Rica's best beaches and mountain resorts is by using unpaved roads. So be careful! While on this subject, let's say a word about potholes. The Costa Rican government tries to keep its paved roads in good shape, but can't keep up with the workload. So watch out for potholes and ruts in the pavement. Your car's shocks and suspension system will be grateful.

For your information there is a new book, "The Essential Road Guide for Costa Rica" by Bill Baker, designed to make driving easier. It is full of common sense rules of the road, maps and a lot of useful data and good advice. This book can be purchased in leading book stores in San José or by contacting Bill Baker, Apartado 1185-1011, San José, Costa Rica or Fax: 220-14-15. If you live in the U.S. or Canada, write to 104 Halfmoon Circle H-3, Hypoluxo, Florida 33462 or call 1-800-881-8607.

If you plan to own your own car, you will need some kind of automobile insurance. Coverage is much more reasonably priced than in the United States. You can purchase your insurance at the I.N.S. (*Instituto National de Seguros*) building, located in downtown San José, or through one of their local agents.

KEEPING YOUR BEARINGS STRAIGHT

If you are going to live in Costa Rica, you can get very confused trying to find your way around, especially in San José. Except for the center of San José, streets don't have names or numbers, and if they do, they are not usually posted in a visible place. People use known landmarks to get around, to locate addresses, and give directions. If you are not familiar with this system it is almost impossible to find your way around and it is easy to get lost. You should not worry because after you have lived in Costa Rica for a while, you will get used to this system. In the event you do happen to get lost, you can always ask Costa Ricans for directions--provided you understand a little Spanish or they speak some English.

As you know, Costa Ricans are generally very friendly, so they will usually be happy to help you find the address you are looking for.

However, it is always a good idea to ask another person because most Ticos are embarassed to admit they don't know an address and sometimes will give you directions whether they know where you want to go or not.

Here are some basic tips on how to get around Costa Rica and understand how the street numbering works. It is somewhat easier to find your way around downtown San José because of the layout of the city. Avenues, or *Avenidas*, run east to west. All the odd numbered avenues are found north of Central Avenue - Avenida Central. The even numbered avenues are to the south. Streets, or *Calles*, run north to south, with odd numbered streets east of Calle Central, and even numbered streets to the west. If you get lost, looking for a street sign on the side of a building and counting by two's will usually help you get your bearings. Keep in mind that the word avenue is often abbreviated as "A" and streets as "C" when you are given written directions.

To find your way around Costa Rica you may need to know that 100 meters (*cien metros*) is another way of saying one block. Likewise, 50 meters (*cincuenta metros*) is a half-block and 150 meters (*ciento cincuenta metros*) a block and a half, etc. . The word *varas* (an old Spanish unit of measurement - almost a yard) is slang and often used instead of the word *metros*-meters, when giving directions. Landmarks such as corner grocery stores (*pulperías*), churches, schools and other buildings are usually used in conjunction with this metric block system to locate addresses. For example, in finding a house someone might say, "From Saint Paul's Church, 200 meters west and 300 south." In interpreting written directions you should also know that "M" stands for meters.

Here is an old trick the Costa Ricans often use for finding the four compass points that might help make it easier for you to find an address or get your bearings straight. The front doors of all churches in Costa Rica face west. So, if there is a church nearby, you will know which way is west, if you can imagine yourself with your back facing the entrance of the church.

Finally, if you live in San José, there is another method for finding the compass points. Use the Volcano Poás for north, the Cruz de Alajuela mountain for approximately south, the direction of Cartago for east and the general direction of the Sabana or Rohrmoser for west. This system of using landmarks should make it easier for you to find you way around the city once you have mastered it.

DOWNTOWN SAN JOSE

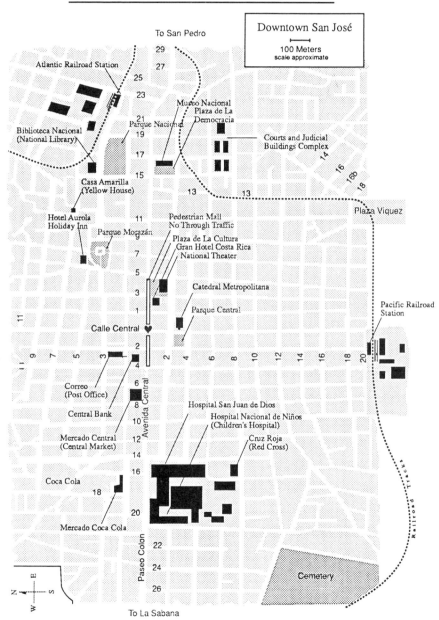

Downtown San José

100 Meters
scale approximate

To San Pedro

Atlantic Railroad Station

Biblioteca Nacional
(National Library)

Museo Nacional
Plaza de La
Democracia

Parque Nacional

Courts and Judicial
Buildings Complex

Casa Amarilla
(Yellow House)

Plaza Viquez

Hotel Aurola
Holiday Inn

Parque Morazán

Pedestrian Mall
No Through Traffic

Plaza de La Cultura
Gran Hotel Costa Rica
National Theater

Catedral Metropolitana

Parque Central

Pacific Railroad
Station

Calle Central

Correo
(Post Office)

Central Bank

Mercado Central
(Central Market)

Hospital San Juan de Dios

Hospital Nacional de Niños
(Children's Hospital)

Cruz Roja
(Red Cross)

Coca Cola

Mercado Coca Cola

Cemetery

Railroad Tracks

Paseo Colon

Avenida Central

To La Sabana

* **Courtesy of Bill Baker**

CHAPTER SIX

Communications

TELEPHONE SERVICES

Costa Rica has the highest number of telephones per capita of any Latin American country and boasts one of the world's best telephone systems, with direct dialing to over 60 countries. Calls within the country are a bargain, since you can call any place in the country for only a few cents. If your house or apartment doesn't have a phone, don't worry. Public telephones are located just about everywhere in Costa Rica and use 5, 10, and 20 colón coins. If you don't have your own phone and want to make a direct international call, you should go to the **RADIOGRAFICA** telephone office, located in downtown San José at Calle 1, Ave. 7, across from the offices of LACSA (open 7 a. m. to 10 p. m.). A collect long distance call can be made from any phone booth by dialing 114. Also, long distance calls can be made from most hotels. As for private phones in homes or offices, again the procedure is just like in the U. S. by direct dialing or first talking to the operator *(OPERADORA)*. The access numbers for calling Costa Rica from abroad are 011-506 plus the rest of the number.

Starting in April of 1994, all phone numbers in Costa Rica will change from six to seven digits. Most phone numbers will have an additional digit before the first number. In some cases the third number will change. A two will be inserted before most numbers in San José. The last four digits of each number will remain the same. We have taken the liberty of inserting most of the new phone numbers in this edition, however, this new system is bound to cause some confusion at first. If you have any problems finding a number, look in the telephone book or dial 113 for assistance, and the operator will help you.

Cellular phone service is also available in Costa Rica. You can call 257-25-27 to get hooked up to the local cellular network.

Sending a FAX is very easy in Costa Rica. You can go to either the *RADIOGRAFICA* (Tel: 287-05-13, 287-05-11) or *TELECOMUNI-CACIONES INTERNCIONALES* (Tel: 257-22-72). At the Radiográfica office you can either send faxes or have faxes sent to you. Also, you can call their office to see if you have received a fax. They will even contact you when a fax comes in if they have your phone number. If you wish many private businesses offer fax services to individuals. You can usually find their number in the classified section of the "Tico Times" or "Costa Rica Today" newspapers.

IMPORTANT TELEPHONE NUMBERS

POLICE 117
PARAMEDICS 118
FIRE DEPARTMENT 118
ELECTRIC COMPANY...126
RURAL GUARD 127
AMBULANCE...128
BILLINGUAL EMERGENCY SERVICE (Like our 911).......122
RED CROSS AMBULANCE 221-58-15
PUBLIC MEDICAL CENTERS:
    HOSPITAL MEXICO................................. 232-61-22
    HOSPITAL NACIONAL DE NIÑOS 222-01-22
    HOSPITAL SAN JUAN DE DIOS 222-01-66
HOSPITAL CALDERON GUARDIA 222-41-33
CLINICA BIBLICA (private hospital with
    24 hour pharmacy) 223-64-22
CLINICA CATOLICA (private hospital) 222-50-55
COLLECT CALLS WITHIN COSTA RICA 110
TIME OF DAY...112
INFORMATION 113
UNLISTED NUMBERS 115
TELEGRAMS..123

MAIL

Costa Rica's postal system or *Cortel* (Correos *y Telégrafos De Costa Rica)* offers postal services comparable to many countries abroad.

Just as in the United States, mail is received and sent from the post office *(correo or casa de correos.)* The main post office is conveniently located in the heart of downtown San José at Calle 2, Ave. 1-3 (223-97-66.) Other small cities and towns in rural areas have their own post offices which are also centrally located. Air mail between the United States or Europe and Costa Rica 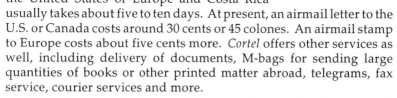 usually takes about five to ten days. At present, an airmail letter to the U.S. or Canada costs around 30 cents or 45 colones. An airmail stamp to Europe costs about five cents more. *Cortel* offers other services as well, including delivery of documents, M-bags for sending large quantities of books or other printed matter abroad, telegrams, fax service, courier services and more.

Please keep in mind that mail boxes are few and far between and house numbers are virtually nonexistent, so we recommend that you use your nearest post office for all postal related matters. Also, we suggest you obtain a post office box *(APARTADO)* from your local post office in Costa Rica to ensure prompt and efficient mail service. To apply for a post office box, go to the post office nearest your office or residence and fill out an application *(SOLICITUD DE APARTADO)*. You will have to pay a small yearly rental fee that ranges between ten to thirty or forty dollars depending on the size of the post office box. These P.O. boxes are in great demand but you can usually get one quite easily in January, when most people give up their leases on their boxes.

Mail may also be received in the general delivery section *(LISTA DE CORREOS)* of your local post office. This is especially useful in an isolated region of the country. All you have to do is register at the nearest post office and they will put your name on the local *lista de correos*. When you pick up your mail you pay a few cents per letter for this service. All letters must have your name, the phrase *lista de correos* and the name of the nearest post office.

A word about having money sent to you in Costa Rica from abroad. There are many ways to receive money while visiting or residing in Costa Rica. The fastest and the safest way is to have an international money order shipped to you via one of the many worldwide courier services, such as DHL or UPS. Letters and small packages usually take about two working days (Mon-Fri) to reach Costa Rica from the United States or Canada. Also, U. S. banks can wire money to the banks in Costa Rica. This method is safe, but there can be many bureaucratic delays while waiting for checks to clear or be processed. The Costa Rican postal service is planning to start a money order service allowing money orders to be sent from the U.S. to Costa Rica. This service promises to be much faster and much more economical than trying to get money wired to your bank in Costa Rica.

Western Union in Costa Rica now boasts that they offer the most rapid money transfer system in the country. They claim that due to their large network of Western Union agencies around the world, they can send money or a message to any person more quickly, securely and easily than their competitors. Call Western Union at 257-13-12 or 257-11-50 for additional information or go to the following agencies located all over the country.

In or near San José:

LOS YOSES - Cambios y Servicios de San José, 20 meters south of the Fátima Church.

TIBAS - Centro Comercial Ana, Carolina #7, 250 west of the Palacio Municipal (city hall)

LA SOEDAD - Contiguo a Tica Bus, Calle 9, Ave. 2 y 4, San José.

ESCAZU - Multiservicios Secretariales, 25 meters east of post office.

In other parts of the country:

LIBERIA - Cambios y Servicios de San José, Agroagencia buildings across from National Bank.

SAN ISIDRO GENERAL - Centro Comercial (shopping center) Placita Pere next to the bank of Costa Rica

PUNTARENAS - Veleros del Sur, S.A. across from the ICE Substation in El Cocal.

There are many money changers *(cambistas)* located in private offices near the central post office and banks in downtown San José. Some of these money changers will often cash your personal checks from your U. S. checking account once they know you well. You can get the name of one of these money changers from other retirees or residents. Social Security and Veteran's benefits can be mailed to you directly through the U.S. Embassy, once you have established a permanent residence in Costa Rica. However, these checks usually don't arrive until sometimes after the tenth of each month.

The worst way to send money is through the regular mail. People report that many checks have been lost or stolen. Postal thieves are very sophisticated in Costa Rica and work in conjunction with some black market money changers. The postal system has received a large number of complaints and has promised to do something about this problem.

If you need to file a complaint about lost or stolen mail, go to *Cortel's Departmento de Reclamaciones* (complaints department) located in downtown San José on Ave. 6, between Calles 17 and 19. If you live outside San José you can file a complaint at any local post office and it will be forwarded to San José.

If you still choose to use the regular mail system after reading the above, be sure to have your checks or money orders sent to you in a security, non-transparent manila envelope - the kind that can't be seen through when held up to a light.

Because of the rash of postal thefts, more and more people are using one of the new private mail companies that offer a variety of postal related services and much more.

Aerocasillas (P.O. Box 4567 -1000, San José, Costa Rica, Tel: 255-45-67, Fax 257-11-87); **Trans-Express "Interlink"** (Tel: 232-25-44); **AAA Express Mail** (Tel: 233-49-93, Fax: 221-50-56); and **Star Box** (P.O. Box 405-1000, San José, Tel: 221-90-29, 221-47-44, Fax: 233-04-48) are a few of the better mail companies which provide clients with a mail drop and P.O. Box in Miami, and a physical address where they can send or receive mail. This enables customers living in Costa Rica to have their mail sent to the Miami address from where the companies forward the mail to Costa Rica. These companies provide much faster service than the Costa Rican mail system to access to mail order products from the U.S., to enable clients to subscribe to magazines and newspapers at U.S. domestic rates, and to help obtain replacement parts from abroad. You can even have your packages picked up and delivered to anyplace, such as your home or office at the time you decide.

Rates run from about 15 to 45 dollars per month depending on the amount of mail you receive and whether you have a business or personal account.

It must be pointed out that the worst time to have any type of correspondence sent to you through the regular Costa Rican mail system is between November 20 and January 1st. Letters can be delayed up to a month because of the enormous volume of Christmas mail and the fact that postal workers are on vacation during part of the month of December. You should avoid having anything larger than a letter or a magazine sent to you in Costa Rica. Any item bigger than that will be sent to the customs warehouse *(ADUANA)* and it will take you several trips to get it out.

On the first trip to customs your package or parcel is unwrapped and you will have to fill out a declaration of what you received. On the second trip you will have to pay the duty. You most certainly will have to pay an exorbitant duty, equivalent to the value of the item plus the mailing cost combined. If you refuse to pay, your package will be confiscated and not sent back to where it came from.

So as you can see, due to the costs involved, it is better to have friends bring you large items, pick them up when visiting the states, or use one of the private mail companies mentioned in this section.

CHAPTER SEVEN

Lodging and Cuisine

HOTELS

While exploring Costa Rica or looking for an apartment, house or some other type of permanent residence, you may choose to stay at one of the many hotels listed below. We have even included aparthotels which are a cross between an apartment and a hotel, as the name implies. If you are only interested in living in Costa Rica on a seasonal basis and not full time, one of these aparthotels is probably your best bet.

We have tried to list a wide range of accomodations to select from. Taking all personal budgets into consideration and have divided them into the following categories according to their approximate rates: Expensive-- $85 and above; Moderately priced-- $35 to $85; Low priced-- below $35; and the Lowest priced-- below $20.

EXCELLENT HOTELS
(Located downtown or near downtown San José.)
AMBASADOR - Moderately priced 221-81-55
BALMORAL - Moderately priced...................................... 222-50-22
CARIARI HOTEL - Expensive, has a golf course 239-00-22
COROBICI - Expensive 232-81-22
EJECUTIVO NAPOLEON - Expensive............................ 223-32-52
EUROPA - Moderately priced 222-12-22
GRAN HOTEL COSTA RICA - Moderately priced 221-40-00

GRAND DE ORO - Expensive (Quaint) 255-33-22
HOTEL AUROLA HOLIDAY INN - Expensive 233-72-33
HOTEL PRESIDENTE - Moderately priced 222-20-34
IRAZU - Moderately priced 232-48-11
L'AMBIANCE - Expensive 223-67-02
LA CASA VERDE DE AMÓN - Moderately priced 223-09-09
PARQUE DEL LAGO - Expensive 222-15-77
SAN JOSE PALACIO - Expensive, newest hotel 220-20-34
TORREMOLINOS - Expensive 222-52-66
VILLA TOURNON - Moderately priced 233-66-22

NICE HOTELS
(Located downtown or near downtown San José.)
AMSTEL - Moderately priced 222-46-22
BOUGAINVILLEA - Moderately priced 233-66-22
DON CARLOS - Moderately priced 221-67-07
GRAN VIA - Moderately priced 222-77-37
HOTEL ROYAL GARDEN - Moderately priced 257-00-22
LA GRAN VIA - Moderately priced 222-77-37
ROYAL DUTCH - Moderately priced 222-14-14
SAN JOSE GARDEN COURT - Moderately priced 255-47-66
TENNIS CLUB - Moderately priced 232-12-66

APARTHOTELS
(Located downtown or near downtown San José.
Some with kitchens, telephones and televisions available)
APARTAMENTOS SCOTLAND - Weekly or monthly 223-08-33
CASTILLA - Moderately low priced 222-21-13
D'GALAH - Moderately low priced .... 234-17-43 or 253-75-39
DON CARLOS - Moderately low priced 221-67-07
EL CONQUISTADOR - Moderately low priced 225-30-22
APARTHOTEL LA SABANA - Moderately priced 220-24-22
RAMGO - Moderately priced 232-38-23
LAMM - Moderately low priced 221-49-20
NAPOLEON - Moderately low priced 223-32-52
RAMGO - Moderately low priced 232-38-23

MORE AFORDABLE PLACES TO STAY
(Located downtown or near downtown San José.
Clean safe rooms - some with meals.)
CASA MARIA DE ESCAZU - Low priced 228-22-70

CASA MARIA DE MORAVIA - Low priced 228-22-70
COSTA RICA INN - Low priced 222-52-03
DIPLOMAT - Low priced 221-81-33
DUNN INN - The best of this group 222-32-32
FORTUNA - Low priced 223-53-44
GALILEA - Low priced 233-69-25
HOTEL ALAMEDA - Low priced 221-30-45
HOTEL CACTS - Budget hotel 221-86-16
HOTEL PARK - Gringo hangout 221-69-44
HOTEL TALAMANCA - Low priced 233-50-33
PETIT HOTEL - Reasonably priced 233-07-66
PICO BLANCO - Low priced, great view 228-31-97
POSADA PEGASUS - Low priced 228-41-96
PLAZA - Low priced 222-55-33
RITZ - Low priced 222-41-03

INEXPENSIVE PLACES TO STAY
(Located downtown or near downtown San José.
* Private baths; ** Some shared)

* ** ASTORIA - The lowest priced 221-21-72
    BELLAVISTA - The lowest priced 223-00-95
 ** BORUCA - The lowest priced 223-00-16
*   CAPITAL - The lowest priced 221-84-97
*   CENTRAL - The lowest priced 221-27-67
*   CORCORI - The lowest priced 233-00-81
*   GRAN HOTEL CENTRAL AMERICA - Good for
    the handicapped 221-33-62
*   HOTEL JOHNSON - Low priced 223-76-33
* ** MARLIN - The lowest priced 233-32-12
    MORAZAN - The lowest priced 221-90-83
    MUSOC - Low priced, next to bus station 222-94-97
 ** TORUMA YOUTH HOSTIL - Inexpensive 222-40-85
 ** TROY'S HOTEL - Located one block east of museum 222-67-56

BED & BREAKFAST
(Small, quaint, and generally, but not necessarily inexpensive,
located downtown or near downtown San José)

HOTEL SAN TOMAS 255-04-48
PENSION DE LA CUESTA 255-28-96
POSADA PEGASUS: ESCAZU 228-41-96
LINDA VISTA LODGE: ESCAZU 228-51-99

GRAN HOTEL COSTA RICA

RESTAURANTS

There are many excellent restaurants, that serve a wide variety of international foods, located all over the San José area. Most of these restaurants are very affordable when compared to similar establishments in the United States. It should be of some comfort to you to know that Costa Rica's restaurants are clean and health codes are strictly enforced by the *Ministerio de* 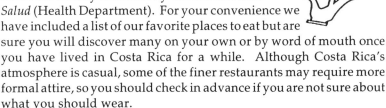 *Salud* (Health Department). For your convenience we have included a list of our favorite places to eat but are sure you will discover many on your own or by word of mouth once you have lived in Costa Rica for a while. Although Costa Rica's atmosphere is casual, some of the finer restaurants may require more formal attire, so you should check in advance if you are not sure about what you should wear.

If you are on a tight budget, try eating at San José's **Central Market** (Calle 6 and Avenida Central). There are 10 to 15 small restaurants, called **sodas**, where a complete meal costs between one and three dollars.

Here are some of San José's most popular dining establishments. Prices vary but in general most are reasonable:

AMSTEL HOTEL: (different cuisines) 233-66-22
BALCON DE EUROPA: (Italian cuisine) 221-48-41
BEIRUT: (Middle East specialties) 257-18-08
CARNES GIGANTES: (specializing in meats) 232-49-69
CHALET SUIZO: (different cuisines) 222-31-18
FLOR DE LOTO: (Hunan & Szechuan Chinese) 232-46-52
GOYA: (Spanish food)
HOTEL BOUGAINVILLA RESTAURANT: (good food) . 233-66-22
LA CASCADA: (Great food, Los Anonos)
LOS ANTOJITOS: (several locations) Mexican food 222-90-86
LA PRINCESA MARINA: (inexpensive seafood)
    Savana Oeste 232-04-81
LOBSTER INN: (seafood, expensive) 223-85-94
LA FUENTE DE MARISCOS: (seafood) 231-06-31
L'ILE: (French) 222-42-41
LA MASIA DE TRIQUELL: (Spanish) 221-50-73
LA NUEVA CHINA: (Chinese) 224-44-78
PAPRIKA: (rich tasting food) 225-89-71

PICCOLA ROMA: (Italian) 223-10-73
RESTAURANT VILLA BONITA: (Best Chinese food
  in San José) 232-98-55
STEAK HOUSE LOS RANCHOS: (Meat dishes,
  Sabana Norte) 232-77-57
VALERIO'S: (Pizza & Lasagne) 225-08-38
VIA VENETO: (Italian) 234-28-98
ZERMATT: (Swiss food) 222-06-04

MORE AFFORDABLE DINING...

CAFE DEL TEATRO NACIONAL: Reasonable prices.
CHARLEY'S BAR AND GRILL: Cajun and North American food.
CHIPS: International food - Plaza de la Cultura.
CONFETTI'S: Nice cafe located across from the Plaza de La ......
  Democracia.
FRIDAYS: Great American style food and "giant" beer mugs.
GRAND DE ORO: Located in a hotel.
HOTEL PICO BLANCO: Great view of San José and very romantic.
JAPPYS: Great desserts.
LA SODA TAPIA: Best breakfasts in San José.
LA CASA DEL ANGEL: Pizza & coffee, inexpensive.
LAS TUNAS: Barbequed beef, seafood, Mexican food and a
  discotheque next door.
LA HACIENDA DE LOS PANCHOS: Authentic Mexican Food.
LA HACIENDA STEAK HOUSE: Dowtown.
LOUISIANA: Cajun-style food on the road to Escazú.
MACCHU PICHU: Peruvian dishes.
MANOLO'S: Good food.
MIRO'S BISTRO: Italian and American.
NOSHERS: Deli and restaurant.
PANADERIA SCHMIDT: Fantastic pastries, Avenida Central.
PIZZA METRO: Unique pizza, downtown.
PIPO'S: Great Sandwiches.
POLLO CAMPESINO: Delicious chicken.
RISAS: Bar and restaurant with American-style food.
ROSTI POLLO: Great chicken cooked over coffee wood, three
  locations.
SODA CENTRAL: Excellent chicken.
SODA PALACE: In the heart of San José.
SPOON: Best of desserts (three locations.)
TEQUILA WILLY'S: Good Tex-Mex food, fun.

TIQUICIA: Typical Costa Rican food and a fantastic wiew of San José.
TORINO: Caribbean style food in Tibás.

VEGETARIAN EATERIES
DITSO: One of San José's newest whole foods restaurants.
DON SOL: Complete cuisine.
LA MACROBIOTICA: Good food.
LA MAZORCA: Great macrobiotic lunches.
EL MORDISCO: Newest veggie cafe in town.
NUTRISODA: Next to Hotel Costa Rica.
SHAKTI: Vegetarian goodies.
VISHNU: Several locations, inexpensive.

FAST FOOD & TAKE OUT
PIZZA HUT (Home delivery available)
Plaza del Sol 253-36-36
La California 255-28-28
Rohrmoser 220-18-18
Escazú 228-98-98
DOMINO PIZZA (Home delivery only)
San Pedro 225-30-30
Centro Comercial Los Anonos 228-95-95
KENTUCKY FRIED CHICKEN
Paseo Colón 222-37-95
Ave Ctl, C 31, Los Yoses 225-98-12
Avenida Segunda 221-83-97
McDONALD'S
Plaza de La Cultura .... Parque de La Paz
Sabana Sur .... Plaza del Sol
Av Ctl, C4 (downtown)
TACO BELL
San Pedro .... La Plaza de La Cultura
BURGER KING
San Pedro .... Sabana Norte (North)
Parque Central .... Diagonal al Edificio de Cristal

CHAPTER EIGHT

Red Tape

DEALING WITH BUREAUCRACY

Just as in the rest of Latin America, Costa Rica is plagued by an inefficient bureaucratic system compared to U. S. standards. This situation is exaggerated by the Latin American temperament, seemingly lackadaisical attitude of most bureaucrats and the generally slower pace of life south of the border. The concept of time is much different than in the U. S. or Canada. When you hear someone say that something will be done "*ahorita*", which literally means right now, you can really expect it to take anywhere from a few minutes to a week, or maybe never. It is not unusual to have to wait in lines for hours in banks and government offices and experience many other unnecessary delays that would almost never occur under similar circumstances in the U. S.

This situation could prove to be very frustrating for foreigners, who are used to fast, efficient service, and it can be especially irritating if you don't speak good Spanish. Since very few people work in the above offices seem to speak fluent English and most North Americans have little knowledge of spoken Spanish, it is advisable to study some basic Spanish. However, if the language proves to be an obstacle at first, we recommend you use a competent bilingual lawyer or see if the *Costa Rican Residents Association* can help you deal with Costa Rica's bureaucracy or "red tape jungle" as it is known. Above all, just learn to be more patient than normal and remember in Costa Rica, just as in the rest of Latin America, you can get the best results from people if you do not push or pressure them.

You shouldn't despair if Costa Rica's "bureaucrazy" gets you down. For a small fee you can also get a person called a *tramitador* to wait in line for you while you tend to some other errand or make better use of your valuable time.

A few words of caution - There are some individuals, who are sometimes called *chorizeros* in popular jargon, who try to pass themselves off as lawyers or who will try to befriend you and offer to help you with red tape, claiming that they can short cut the bureaucratic system because of their contacts. A general rule of thumb is to avoid such individuals or you will end up losing valuable time, run the risk of acquiring forged documents; most certainly lose money, and experience a lot of grief. Also, since bribery is an institution in most Latin American countries and the majority of government employees are underpaid, some people will advise you to pay extra money to speed up paper work or circumvent normal channels. This practice of bribery is illegal and not recommended for foreigners, since they can be deported for breaking the law. However, in some instances it may be necessary to pay extra money to get things done. Use your own discretion in such matters.

Finally, while we are on the subject of bureaucracy, all persons planning to live or retire in Costa Rica should know that the American Embassy, located in the San José suburb of Pavas, can help with the following: Social Security and Veterans benefits, getting documents notarized, obtaining a new U. S. passport, registering the births of your children abroad, getting a U.S. visa for your spouse (if you chose to marry a Costa Rican), obtaining an absentee ballot to vote in U.S. elections and U.S. income tax forms and information. We would like to point out that if you get into any kind of legal trouble in Costa Rica, you should not expect too much help from the U.S. Embassy.

HOW TO BECOME A LEGAL RESIDENT OF COSTA RICA

If you plan to live in Costa Rica for no more than six months a year, you can do so by getting extensions on your visa. Tourists may remain in the country for six months legally without having to apply for permanent residency. You may even own property, start some type of business or make other types of investments with nothing more than a tourist visa. We know many Americans, Canadians and other foreigners who have started businesses as tourists. However, if you plan to reside in Costa Rica full-time, one of Costa Rica's permanent residency programs is the best way to go.

There are several residency categories available that will permit you to maintain your current citizenship and obtain long-term legal status in Costa Rica: *resident pensionado, pensionado rentista,* and *rentista inversionista* (resident investor). Whatever program you choose depends on your particular needs and financial position.

Before making your choice you should know that in March of 1992 the pensionado law was changed eliminating many of the tax privileges that retirees enjoyed since the program was started in 1964.

Under the old system foreigners with official *pensionado or rentista* (permanent retiree) status, were required to reside in the country for four months a year, and were entitled to the following perks: Permanent residency without immigration hassles; all the privileges of a Costa Rican citizen, except the right to vote and work for hire; one of each duty-free major appliance such as a refrigerator, a stove, a microwave, a television, a washer and dryer, and many unlimited personal household goods. *Pensionados* were also permitted to bring a new car into the country every five years without having to pay normal duties, provided it was worth less than $16,000.00. In 1992, the two most worthwhile exonerations were eliminated: Low taxes on an imported cars and duty free household goods. Since then, all new *pensionados* have to pay the same taxes on their automobiles and household goods as ordinary Costa Rican citizens. The rest of the *pensionado's* privileges remain pretty much intact, the most notable of which is permanent residency whereby you can stay in the country legally. So, we suggest you consider these facts before deciding if it is advantageous for you to become a *pensionado*.

Despite the apparent shortcommings of the new law, many retirees will still find Costa Rica an attractive retirement haven since the country has so much to offer. People continue to flock to Costa Rica because of the peaceful atmosphere, excellent climate, friendly people, natural beauty and so much more we have mentioned and not because of tax exonerations on a few luxury items. In addition, there is a good chance that the Costa Rican government has reduced some taxes on cars and other formerly taxed imported goods, making them affordable to most Costa Ricans as well as foreign residents, thus eliminating the need for any type of tax exoneration program.

If it is absolutely necessary to have an automobile, you can always bring one from the states that is five years or older and only pay a couple of thousand dollars in taxes on it. You can also go to the "free port" of Golfito in southern Costa Rica, where a stove, refrigerator or other appliances can be purchased without paying high import duties.

It should be of some comfort to any person thinking about becoming a *pensionado* that a lawsuit has been filed on behalf of the *pensionados*, by the *Pensionado* Association, now called the **Costa Rican Residents Association**, in response to the elimination of their tax privileges. Also, there are many rumors circulating that after the presidential elections in 1994, many of the pensionado's perks will be restored. So, there is now a glimmer of hope that this law will be changed. On a more encouraging note, in mid-1993, all persons who were *pensionados* prior to April 1992, regained some of their rights and privileges as a result of a court decision.

Now let's look at the requirements and specific documents that you will need to present to the Costa Rican government if you should choose to apply for either the *resident pensionado, pensionado rentista* categories.

A **RESIDENT PENSIONADO** is someone who lives off a pension like a U.S. Social Security check or some type of permanent retirement program. A husband and wife cannot combine their pensions but the wife can live under the husband's *pensionado* status or visa versa. If the recipient of the pension passes away, the other spouse can retain the *pensionado* status if he or she inherits the pension. However, there is some paper work involved.

Here are the requirements for this category:

Resident Pensionado
1. A lifetime income of at least $600 a month generated from outside of Costa Rica.
2. A signed letter confirming that you will receive this money in Costa Rica.
3. A letter from a C.P.A. stating that you will receive the $600 for life, if the pension comes from a company's pension plan.
4. If the money comes from a company, two letters from bank officials showing that your company is financially sound and the pension plan must have been in existance for at least 20 years .
5. A detailed account of your company's pension plan.

As a *pensionado* you are also obligated to change $7,200 ($600 per month) a year into colones at a government bank. You need to do this to update your file. If you can't prove that you have converted your money you can lose your status. You also have to renew your *pensionado* I.D. card every couple of years and as you know, reside in the country for at least four months yearly. Finally, as a *pensionado* you can own and operate your own business.

PENSIONADO RENTISTA is another kind of residency category designed for those who are not retired and don't receive any type of government pension. To qualify for *rentista* status, an applicant must have an income of $12,000 a year ($1,000 per month) that has to come from some type of investment or annuity. As a *rentista* you must prove that this investment will be stable for at least five years. At the end of five years you have to prove the validity of your source of income all over again. Furthermore, every year as a *rentista* you have to prove you have changed $12,000 into colones and show your passport to prove that you were in the country for at least four months.

As a *pensionado rentista* you can also own and operate a business. The only apparent disadvantage to this particular program is that you have to tie up your funds for five years.

In brief to qualify for ***pensionado rentista status*** you need:
1. An income of $1,000 per month for the next five years in Costa Rica.
2. If the income is from a foreign source you need documentation that attests to the company or bank's solvency.

RENTISTA INVERSIONISTA is another permanent resident status for those people who are not retired and want to invest in Costa Rica. If you have a lot of money to invest, this might be the best route to go. The goverrnment will grant residency under this category to anyone who invests at least $50,000 in high priority projects like tourism, reforestation or $200,000 in any other business. The amount of paperwork and requirements are similar to the other residency programs, in that certain documentation has to be provided. Since every circumstance is different, we suggest you contact the Residents Association or a good lawyer to clear up any confusion that might arise.

The following other documents are required for both the *pensionado, rentista, rentista-inversionista* (resident investor) and any other residency categories:
1. An application to the Director of Intelligence and Security.
2. Medical examinations performed by the corresponding departments of the ministry of Public Health of Costa Rica.

3. The formal application should have the following information: full name, nationality, passport number, dependents, date of entry into Costa Rica, origin of income and the amount, address in country of origin or Costa Rica; authentication by a notary public and corresponding stamps.

4. **A sworn notarized declaration:** Stating that you won't work in Costa Rica; that if you leave the country you will notify I.C.T.; that you will spend 4 months a year in Costa Rica; that you have no police record; that you will change the required number of dollars per month at a national bank.

5. **Police Certificate** from your local area stating that you have no record. (This document is only good for 6 months, so make sure it is current.)

6. **Birth Certificate**

7. **Marriage certificate** if applicable

8. **Certified copy** of your entire passport

9. **Certificate of non-residence**

10. **Twelve passport size photos** -- 6 front view and 6 profile

If you meet the prerequisites to qualify for any of the residency categories and have received all of the above documents, you are now ready to formally apply for your chosen status. The next step is to have the Costa Rican Residents Association or an attorney of your choice, present your papers to the tourist board (I.C.T.), who will then process them in approximately a couple of months.

If you want to avoid dealing with the many inconveniences of Costa Rica's giant "bureaucrazy" and save time and money in the long run, we suggest you join the **Costa Rican Residents Association**. This excellent organization was formerly called the Pensionado Association, but changed its name as of July of 1992 due to changes in the *pensionado* law. The association has been reorganized and to some extent revitalized, and now offers services to all legal residents in Costa Rica and not just the *pensionados* as before.

For a small membership fee of $50, the Costa Rican Residents Association, conveniently located in the I.C.T. building on Avenida 4 at Calle 5 diagonal to the national theater, will assist you with the following if you need help: applying for *pensionado* or any other residency status ($1,000)- (a good deal since many lawyers can charge up to $2,000 for the same service and take much longer) buying and selling cars, and help you get a Costa Rican driver's license (see chapter 5 for details); assist with English to Spanish translations of any required documents and papers; make sure your annual papers are up-to-date; notarize all your important documents; help with the renewal of your I.D. card or *cédula* and show you how to obtain medical coverage offered by the Costa Rican Social Security System and the new supplemental coverage that they (The Residents Association) now offers (see the section on medical care for the details). Should you desire additional information, contact:

Costa Rican Resident's Association

Apartado 700-1011

San José, Costa Rica

Call: 333-80-68 inside Costa Rica and 011-506-333-80-68 if you are outside of the country. Fax 011 (506) 222-78-62.

Address in the U.S. for your convenience:

Costa Rican Resident's Association

P.O. Box 025292-SB19

Miami, Florida 33102-5292

or contact:

Departamento de Rentistas

Instituto Costarricense de Turismo

Apartado, 777-1000

San José, Costa Rica

Tel: 011-506-223-17-33, Ext. 264

ADDITIONAL METHODS OF OBTAINING COSTA RICAN RESIDENCY

As we mentioned in the last section, since most of the *pensionado* programs attractive privileges were removed in 1992, the only real advantage to becoming a *pensionado* is to use it as a vehicle for staying in the country legally. Consequently, more and more people are looking at alternative ways of obtaining Costa Rican residency.

Basically, the residency program is for those people who want to reside in Costa Rica on a full-time basis but cannot qualify for *pensionado* or *rentista* status, or those who can qualify, but choose not to do so because some of the attractive perks were taken away as we just alluded to.

There are several other ways that foreigners can obtain legal residency. As we mentioned in the last section, they can become a

Residente Inversionista (resident investor) by investing $50,000 in a priority project such as reforestation, tourism, exports or $200,000 in anything else. They can also claim residency because they have an immediate relative in Costa Rica - a child, a spouse or parent, and they can prove they have the financial means to support themselves while living in Costa Rica (about $600 per month). In addition, if they have lived for at least two years under another residency category, such as *pensionado* or *rentista*, they can apply for Costa Rican residency. Many ex-*pensionados* are doing the latter, because they can generally qualify for this status easily. With this type of residency you have to reside in the country six months a year.

Temporary residency, *residencia temporal*, may be obtained by students who are enrolled in a university or language school, by Peace Corps volunteers, and by members of affiliated church service groups. Language teachers at any of the many language institutes in San José may obtain a type of temporary residency that enables them to stay in the country legally. Others who can do jobs that Costa Ricans cannot do are also eligible for this status.

Because each person's situation is different, the procedure is complicated. As with the other residency programs there is a lot of paper work, we advise you to consult a lawyer to facilitate this process. To find a competent, trustworthy attorney, it is best to go to the Costa Rican Residents Association office and read the section in this chapter titled, "How to Find a Lawyer."

There is an additional way to acquire residency for those foreigners who have resided in Costa Rica since July 31, 1993 and don't have a criminal record. They may now apply for Costa Rican residency to get a *cédula* (residency card). This may be done during the amnesty period that lasts until mid-April of 1993.

Most of the readers of this book will not qualify for this special residency program, but we thought that it deserved mention in this section.

IMMIGRATION AND OTHER MATTERS

"PERPETUAL TOURIST"

If you don't want to hassle becoming a *pensionado* or resident, you can live as a perpetual tourist in Costa Rica. There is no paper work or lawyers involved. Just leave the country every three months to renew your tourist visa. All you have to do is leave the country for at least 72 hours. You can repeat this process over-and-over again to stay in Costa indefinitely. The only disadvantage is that as a tourist you can't work in Costa Rica and it is almost impossible to become a legal resident, unless you marry a Costa Rican or have immediate Costa Rican relatives.

If you don't want to bother leaving the country every few months to renew your papers, you can stay in the country illegally, but will have to pay a small fine when you eventually do leave. The fine is about five dollars a month. We have personally met many people who have been living as tourists for years without any hassles and even started businesses. Bear in mind that it is always better to have your papers up-to-date because if you get into any kind of trouble you can be deported almost "on the spot" if you are found to be in the country illegally.

EXTENDING TOURIST CARDS

Every tourist is given permission to remain in Costa Rica for ninety days. To extend their stay, tourists must apply for an extension, called a *PRORROGA*, prior to the end of their first ninety days in the country. A tourist is usually entitled to one of two such extensions, depending on the circumstances of the request. The new immigration offices are located in the suburb of La Uruca, near the Irazú Hotel and LACSA's main offices. Most travel agencies can help extend tourist cards and/or exit visas for a small fee. This method helps you avoid long lines and saves you valuable time.

LEAVING THE COUNTRY

Any tourist who has stayed in Costa Rica for more than thirty days must get a *PENSION ALIMENTICIA* document at the Supreme Court building and an *EXIT VISA* at the immigration office in order to leave the country. Costa Rican citizens, retirees and permanent residents must also do the same. If you are a foreigner, living under one of the three residency categories your resident's exit visa, will cost about $40.00.

CHILDREN'S EXIT VISAS

Children under 18, of all nationalities even infants, are not allowed to remain in Costa Rica for more than thirty days unless both parents request permission from the National Child Welfare Agency *(Patronato Nacional de la Infancia)* for the child to leave the country. One parent or guardian cannot get permission without written permission from the non-accompanying other parent. This document has to be notarized by a Costa Rican consul in the child's home country. If you don't adhere to this procedure, your child will not be able to leave the country. A travel agent or lawyer may be able to get permission from the *Patronato* if you give them the child's passport and two extra Costa Rican-sized passport photos.

COSTA RICAN CITIZENSHIP

After living in Costa Rica for a number or years many foreigners decide for one reason or another that they want to acquire Costa Rican citizenship. If you can qualify, this is another way to stay in the country legally. From what we have been told, if you have lived in Costa Rica for more than two years under any of the permanent residency programs, you may apply for Costa Rican citizenship. The only disadvantage is that you may have to relinquish your original citizenship. As far as we know, the U.S. does not allow for dual citizenship. However, we know of a number of North Americans who have both U.S. and Costa Rican citizenship. One expat we know uses the Costa Rican passport for travel, only because he claims there are less problems than with a U.S. passport. We suggest you consult an attorney for all the details and specific requirements if you are interested in this category.

GETTING MARRIED

Getting married in Costa Rica is really quite simple. All you have to do is complete the required paperwork and have the appropriate documents like a passport, divorce papers (if you were previously married) and any other pertinent information. We suggest you consult your lawyer if you are thinking of marrying someone in Costa Rica to find out exactly what documents you need to have and what procedures you have to follow.

By the way, lawyers can marry people in Costa Rica much like a justice of the peace in the states. This type of marriage is called *por civil*, and is usually quicker than a traditional church wedding or *por la iglesia*. In Costa Rica many people get married both ways.

If you do choose to have a lawyer marry you, you will have to round up a couple of witnesses for the ceremony.

BRINGING AN AUTOMOBILE
TO COSTA RICA

There are two ways to bring a car to Costa Rica - by sea or by land. If you choose to have your car shipped to Costa Rica by boat you should contact a shipping company near to where you have your vehicle in the U.S. or one of the companies we mention in the next section of this book. This method of transportation is relatively safe since your car travels by ship and you can insure it against all types of possible damage. Depending on where you ship your car from in the United States or Canada, your vehicle should not take more than a month to reach Costa Rica, if you have all of your paperwork in order. The cost can range from a few hundred dollars to over a thousand dollars depending on the port of departure. One of the advantages of sending your car this way is that you can sometimes load it with your small household goods so that you won't have to send them separately. Don't forget to inventory and insure these items. Some cars have arrived stripped of their contents.

If you have a lot of time on your hands and like adventure, you can drive your automobile to Costa Rica. The journey from the U.S. to Costa Rica, depending on the point along the U.S.-Mexican border where you choose to enter, can be made in about three weeks if you drive at a moderate speed. (The shortest distance from the U.S. to Costa Rica by land is 2250 miles through Brownsville, Texas). It is best to take your time so you can stop and see some of the sights. This way you can rest and will only have to drive during the day. We recommend driving only during the day since most roads are poorly lighted at night and large animals like cows, donkeys and horses can stray onto the road at anytime and cause a serious accident.

It is important that your car be in good mechanical condition before you undertake your trip. Carry necessary spare tires and parts. You should also have a can of gas and try to keep your gas tank as full as possible since service stations can be few and far between.

Be sure that all your documents such as visas and passports are in order well in advance to avoid problems at border crossings. Remember, passports are required for all U.S. citizens driving through Central America. You also need to have complete car insurance, a valid driver's license and a vehicle registration. You can purchase insurance from AAA in the U.S., or another type of insurance by contacting Sanborn's Insurance in the U.S. (512) 686-0711, or buy it at the border before entering Mexico. If you are missing any of these items, border guards can make your life miserable. Some border crossings close down at night so you should plan to arrive at all borders between 8 a.m. and 5 p.m., just to be safe.

When you finally do arrive at the Costa Rican border from Nicaragua, you may be delayed for some time clearing customs, especially if you are bringing a lot of personal possessions from the U.S. with the intention of living in Costa Rica permanently. Some or all of these items might be inventoried and taken to the custom's warehouse in San José where you must pick them up at a later date, once you have paid the necessary taxes.

It is our understanding that a tourist may keep a car in the country for up to three months. An additional three-month extension can be applied for and is usually granted, but after a total of six months the vehicle will have to be taken out of the country or it will be taxed. However, any person who brings a car to Costa Rica by land or sea, and pays all of the taxes, may keep the a car in the country indefinitely once all the necessary paperwork has been completed.

If you do decide that you want to keep your vehicle in Costa Rica, here is a simple formula for figuring out how much you will have to pay in taxes. You pay 100 percent of the value of a new car and 60 percent of the value of a new pickup truck, plus the value of those shipping charges. If the car is a year old, you get a 20% discount. You get a 10% discount for the second, third and fourth years. For example, on a five year old car you pay taxes on 30% of the value. The value is the manufacturer's suggested retail price. This means if you have a five-year old car that is valued at $9,000 and you paid $1,000 to ship it, you owe the customs $3,000.

Those of you who would like additional information on driving from the U.S. to Costa Rica, can purchase a new guide book, "Driving the Panamerican Highway to Mexico and Central America," by writing: Interlink 209, P.O. Box 526-770 Miami, FL. 33152, if you live outside of Costa Rica. If you currently reside in Costa Rica, you can write to: Ray Prichard, Marketing Consultants, APDO 208-3000, Heredia, Costa Rica, C.A. The price of this book is $13.00 plus $2.50 for postage and handling.

SHIPPING YOUR HOUSEHOLD GOODS TO COSTA RICA

As previously stated, the old *pensionado* program enabled retirees to import many household items including an automobile virtually duty-free. Since most of these privileges have been rescinded, you might have second thoughts about importing any of said items. You shouldn't worry because many of these goods, or a similar product may be puchased in Costa Rica. They usually cost more than in the U. S., except at the free port of Golfito in southern Costa Rica, because they are imported. Also, the selection is not nearly as good and the quality of some local items leaves a lot to be desired.

To save time and money, it is best to purchase these goods in Los Angeles, Houston, New Orleans or preferably Miami. The latter is the nearest U.S. port of departure to Costa Rica and shipping costs are even lower. You can look in the yellow pages of the Miami phone book to locate a shipping company or contact one of the companies we have listed below. We understand that there are also some trucking companies that will ship your belongings overland.

It must be pointed out that after taking high shipping costs into consideration, you may be reluctant to ship any household items from the U.S. this is a matter of personal choice. Most foreign residents and even Costa Ricans prefer U.S. products because of their higher quality. Many retirees live comfortably and happily without some or any luxuries and expensive appliances. You can rent a furnished apartment or if you chose, furnish an unfurnished apartment, excluding stove and refrigerator, for a few hundred dollars. What you need to import really depends on your personal lifestyle and budget.

Here are some money saving tips for bringing your household goods to Costa Rica. First, if you enter the country as a tourist by plane, you can usually bring in a lot of personal effects and small appliances. As a tourist sometimes you are even waved through customs without ever having to open any of your luggage. You can also have friends bring a few things to you when they visit you in Costa Rica. Any way you look at it, you should always try to take as much with you as you can by plane rather than shipping items by boat, because most used personal items are not taxed at the airport. Even used appliances have a good chance of clearing airport customs if you can fit them on the plane. You should make an effort to get rid of "clutter" and not ship anything that you can easily or cheaply replace in Costa Rica. You should also make a point of talking to other retirees to find out what they think is absolutely necessary to bring to Costa Rica.

If you chose to send some of your possessions by ship, once they arrive in Costa Rica you will have to exercise extreme patience and be prepared to face many unnecessary delays and frustrations when dealing with the Costa Rican custom's house, or *aduana* as it is called. It is not unusual to have to make many trips to the custom's warehouse to get your belongings. You may spend all day going from window to window and dealing with mountains of paperwork, only to be told at the end of the day that you have to come back the following morning to pick up your belongings. Futhermore, fickle customs officials decide the value of the shipped goods and two identical shipments, can have completely different tax amounts, depending who examines them at the *aduana*.

Because of this dilatory process, many people pay a local customs broker, *Agencia Aduanera*, or hire some other person like their lawyer to do this unpleasent task for them. It may cost you a little more this way, but it will save you valuable time. For additional information contact by phone or write:

Worldwide Movers Air and Sea Freight
P.O. Box 253-1007
Centro Colón
San José, Costa Rica
Fax (506) 233-0517
Tel: 011-506-233-4785
Servex Inernational S.A.
P.O.Box 1285-1000
San José, Costa Rica
Tel: 011-506-53-1152
Fax 506-224-8437

Consult the yellow pages for listing of Agencias Aduaneras (Custom's brokers). The Pensionado Association suggests you contact moving expert, Carlos Bravo before you decide to ship your belongings to Costa Rica. Tel: 255-11-52, Fax: 224-84-37.

HOW TO FIND A LAWYER

If you plan to go into business, work, buy or sell property and/or seek long-term residence status, you will certainly need the services of a good attorney. Your attorney can also help you understand the complexities of the Costa Rican legal system, which is based on Roman law and does not work like our system in the United States. He can assist you with bureaucratic procedures and handle any other legal matters that might arise.

As you already know, the lawyer you chose, as well as his secretary should be bilingual (Spanish/English). This will help you avoid communication problems, misunderstandings, and enable you to stay on top of your legal affairs. It is very important to watch your lawyer closely, since most Costa Rican lawyers tend to drag their feet like bureaucrats. Never take for granted that things are getting done. Check with your lawyer on a regular basis and ask to see your file to make sure he has taken care of you business. As you know paper work is slow moving in Costa Rica, and you don't want to protract the process any more than you have to. Also, be sure your lawyer is accessible at all hours. You should have his office telephone number and his home number in case you have to locate him if there is an emergency. If your lawyer is always in meetings or out of the office this is a clear sign that your work is being neglected and you have chosen the wrong lawyer. You should also make sure you know your lawyer's specialty. Although most attorneys are required to have a general knowledge of Costa Rican law, you may need a specialist to deal with your specific case. Some retirees have found it is a good idea to have several lawyers for precisely this reason.

It is best to take your time and look around when you are trying to find a good lawyer. Ask other retirees and knowledgeable people for the names of their lawyers, and then try to find out as much as you can about your potential lawyer's reputation and how he works. If you find yourself in a jam, you can contact the *Residents Association* or go to one of the many lawyer's offices located in the vicinity of the courthouse. Like everywhere else in the world, there are always some incompetent, unscrupulous attorneys, so it is best to know who you are dealing with before you make you final choice. Remember, one of the most important and valuable persons you will be associated with while living in Costa Rica is your lawyer, so it is of utmost importance that you develop a good working relationship.

It is not advisable to select a lawyer solely on the basis of legal fees. Lawyers fees, or *honorarios*, vary. Just because a lawyer charges a lot doesn't mean he is good. Likewise you shouldn't choose an attorney because his fees are low. However, if you can find a competent lawyer who will handle your *pensionado* paperwork for under $1,000 you are getting a good deal. You can check with the

Costa Rican equivalent of the Bar Association *(El Colegio de Abogados)* if you have any questions about legal fees.

You will be happy to know that in Costa Rica it is surprisingly more affordable than you think to hire a lawyer on a full time basis, by paying what amounts to a small retainer. You should also know that there is a small amount of paper work involved to give your lawyer "power of attorney", *poder*, so he or she can take care of your personal business and legal affairs. This is not a bad idea if you ever have to leave the country for a period of time or in the event of an emergency. However, first make sure your lawyer is completely trustworthy and competent in such matters.

COSTA RICAN CONSULATES AND EMBASSIES ABROAD

Anyone who wants to become a retiree or seeks permanent residency in Costa Rica will have to have certain documents notarized by a Costa Rican consulate or embassy in their country of origin. Some of the documents that may need to be notarized are: a birth certificate, police certificate (stating you have no criminal record) and proof of income statement. It is recommended that all this paper work be taken care of before coming to Costa Rica.

If you apply for any type of permanent residency status from Costa Rica it may take months for you to get the required notarized documents from your home country. If worse comes to worse you may even have to make an unnecessary trip home to take care of these matters. Also, while you are waiting for your papers from abroad some of the other documents may expire and you will have to go through the process all over again. Bureaucracy is slow enough as it is in Costa Rica, and it is foolish to delay this process any more than necessary.

Here are some of the Costa Rican Consulates and Embassies abroad:

Consulates in the United States:

Atlanta: 315 West Ponce de Leon, Suite 455, Decatus, GA 30030
Tel: (404) 370-0555, FAX: (404) 377-7992

Boston: 672 Chesnut Hill, Brookline, MA 02146
Tel: (617) 738-9708

Buffalo: 5370 Siegle Road, Lockport, NY 14094

Chicago: 8 S. Michigan Ave., Suite 1312, Chicago, Ill. 60603

Dallas: 4100 Traris Street, Suite 202, Dallas, TX 75204

Denver: 1633 Filmore Street, Denver, CO 80206, Tel: (303) 778-6032, FAX: (303) 377-0050

Hawaii: 819 Koto Isle Circle, Honolulu, HI 96825

Houston: 3000 Wilcrest, Suite 145, Houston, Tx. 77042

Kansas City: 416 West 61st Street, Kansas City, MO 64113

Las Vegas: P.O. Box 80494, Las Vegas, NV 89180
Tel: (702) 363-2925

Los Angeles: 3540 Wilshire Blvd., Suite 404, Los Angeles, CA 90010
Tel: (213) 380-7915, FAX: (213) 289-1245

Miami: Consulate General, 1600 N.W. Le Jeune Rd., 3rd Floor
Miami, FL 33126, Tel: (305) 871-7485, FAX: (305) 871-0860

Milwaukee: 130 Lexington Blvd., White Fish Bay, WI 53217
Tel: (414) 332-0376

New Jersey: 45 Summer Street, Passaic, NJ 07055

New Mexico: 4033 Luelle Anne, Albuquerque N.M. 87109

New Orleans: Consulate General Costa Rica, 2002 Street 20th,
Suite B-103, Kenner, LA 70062, Tel: (504) 467-1462, FAX: (504) 466-8268

New York: 80 S. Wall Street, Suite 1117, New York, NY 10005

Orlando: 401 E. Jackson Street, Suite 204 , Orlando, FL 32801
Tel: (407) 422-4544, FAX: (407) 422-5220

Philadelphia: 335 E. Main Street, Morrestown, PA 08057
Tel: (609) 235-6277

Pittsburgh: 1164 Harvard Road, Monroeville, PA 15146
Tel: (412) 856-7967

Portland: 2050 N.W. Love Joy, Portland, OR 97209, (503) 224-0103

Raleigh: 2301 Stonehenge Drive, Suite 2, Raleigh, NC 27015
Tel: (919) 676-1422, FAX: (919) 676-9734

Salt Lake City: 751 South 300 E., Salt Lake City, UT 84111,
Tel: (801) 753-3490/6545

San Antonio: Continental Bldg., 6836 San Pedro, Suite 206B
San Antonio, TX 78216, Tel: (512) 824-8489, FAX: (512) 829-5553
San Diego: P.O. Box 880-695, San Diego, CA 92108,
Tel: (619) 277-9447, FAX: (619) 563-1059

San Francisco: 870 Market Street, Suite 548, San Francisco, CA 94102
Tel: (415) 392-8488, FAX: (415) 392-3745

St. Louis: 7700 Bonhomme, Suite 200, Saint Louis, MO 63105
Tel: (314) 725-1200, FAX: (314) 725-3227

St. Paul: 2400 Kasota Avenue, St. Paul, MN 55108, Tel: (612) 645-3401,
FAX: (612) 645-7444

Vancouver: 8500 N.E. Hazel Dell Ave J-11, Vancouver, WA 98665
Tel: (206) 576-0710, FAX: (503) 693-0623

Washington, D.C.: 1825 Connecticut Ave. N.W., Suite 211
Washington, D.C. 20009, Tel: (202) 234-2945, FAX: (202) 234-2946

Consulates Abroad:

England
14 Lancaster Gate
London, England
K2P 1B7

Canada
Embassy of Costa Rica
135 York Street, Suite 208
Ottawa, Ontario K1N 5T4
Tel: (613) 562-2855
FAX: (613) 562-2582

Canada
614 Centre A. Street N.W.
Calgary, Alberta
Canada

Canada
7 Lia Crescent Don Mills
Toronto, Ontario
Canada

Canada
1520 Alberni Street
Vancouver, B.C.
Canada

Canada
1155 Dorchester Blvd. W.
Suite 2902, Montreal
P.Q. H3B2L3
Canada

EMBASSIES AND CONSULATES IN COSTA RICA

If you are planning to travel and explore Latin America and other parts of the world, once you are settled in Costa Rica, you will need the addresses of the embassies and consulates listed below in order to get visas and other necessary travel documents.

Argentina, Ave 6 Calle 21-25 221-68-69

Austria (consulate) Ave. 4 Calle 36-38 255-07-67

Belgium, Los Yoses 225-62-55

Belize, Guadalupe 253-96-26

Bolivia, Ave Central, Calle 9-12 233-62-44

Brazil, Ave. 2, Calle 20-22 233-15-44

Canada, Ave ct. 1 Calle 3 255-35-22

Chile, Barrio Dent 224-42-43

China, San Pedro 224-81-80

Columbia, Ave. 1, Calle 29 221-07-25

Ecuador (consulate) Paseo Colón, Calle 38-40 226-62-82

El Salvador, Los Yoses 225-38-61, 224-90-34

France, Curridabat 225-07-33

Germany, Ave 5, Calle 40-42 232-55-33

Great Britain, Paseo Colón 221-55-66

Guatemala, (consulate) Barrio California 233-52-83

Honduras Los Yoses 234-09-49, 222-21-45

Italy, Los Yoses, Ave 10, Calle 33-35 234-23-26

Israel, Ave, 2-4, Calle 2 221-60-11

Jamaica (consulate) Urb. Los Anonos 228-08-02

Japan, Rohrmoser 232-12-55

MexicoBarrio Armon 222-55-28, 232-24-56

Nicaragua, Barrio California 233-34-79

Panamá, San Pedro 225-34-01

ParaguaySan Ramón - Tres Rios 233-37-94, 225-28-02

Perú, Los Yoses 225-91-45

Puerto Rico, Ave 2, Calle 11-13 257-17-69

Spain, Ave. 2 (Paseo Colón) Calle 32 222-19-33

Switzerland, Paseo Colón, Calle 38-40 233-00-52

Taiwan, Guadalupe 224-49-92

United States of America, Pavas - Rohrmoser 220-39-39

Uruguay, Los Yosas 234-99-09, 223-25-12

U.S.S.R., Curridabat 272-10-21, 225-57-80

Venezuela, Los Yoses 225-58-13

CHAPTER NINE

Other Useful

Information

9.

COSTA RICA'S POTABLE WATER

Unlike other countries in Latin America, especially Mexico, Costa Rica's water supply is good and perfectly safe to drink in San José and in the majority of small towns. In most places, you can drink water without fear of "Montezuma's Revenge" (dysentery) or other intestinal problems. However, be careful when you drink water in the countryside. We have lived in Costa Rica for years and not heard many people complain about the quality of Costa Rica's water. But if you prefer, bottled water is available. You will be pleased to know that Costa Rica's water is also soft for bathing purposes.

FRUITS, VEGETABLES AND OTHER BARGAIN FOODS

There is a wide variety of delicious tropical fruits and vegetables in Costa Rica. As a matter of fact it is amazing that there are every imaginable fruit and vegetable you can think of plus some exotic native varieties. More common tropical fruits such as pineapples, mangos and papayas cost about a third of what they do in the United States. Bananas can be purchased at any local fruit stand or street market for about five cents each.

Once you have lived in Costa Rica you can do like many Costa Ricans and eat a few slices of mouth-watering fruit for breakfast at one of the many sidewalk *fruterías* or fruit stands located all over the country. For people who are living on a tight budget, this type of healthy fresh fruit breakfast will cost you about 50 or 60 cents. There are also many *sodas,* or small cafes, where you can eat a more typical Costa Rican breakfast for around a dollar.

Besides fruits and vegetables there are many other bargain foods available in Costa Rica. Bakeries sell fresh home-made breads 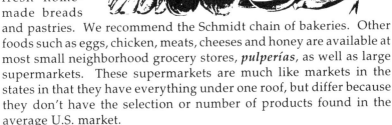 and pastries. We recommend the Schmidt chain of bakeries. Other foods such as eggs, chicken, meats, cheeses and honey are available at most small neighborhood grocery stores, *pulperías,* as well as large supermarkets. These supermarkets are much like markets in the states in that they have everything under one roof, but differ because they don't have the selection or number of products found in the average U.S. market.

Many prepackaged imported products can be found in Costa Rican supermarkets but are very expensive. It is not unusual to pay double for a box of your favorite breakfast cereal, certain canned foods or liquor. You don't have to worry because there are some local products you can substitute for your favorite U.S. brand. However, if you find you absolutely cannot live without your prepackaged foods from the states, you can usually find the product you are looking for at Bubis imported food stores or at one of the Auto Mercados supermarkets perhaps at a very high price. If you want to save money, we suggest you stock-up on these items while on a shopping trip to the states and bring them with you by plane when you return to Costa Rica. You can also have friends or relatives bring you the food items you need when they visit. If you ever go to the neighboring country of Panama you will find many American food products sold there.

Since most foods are so affordable in Costa Rica, you will be better off if you try changing your eating habits and buy more local products or substitutes, so you can keep your food bill low. You can further save money by shopping at the Central Market, *Mercado Central ,* like many cost-conscious Costa Ricans. The market covers a whole city block and is located in the heart of downtown San José, near the banking district. Everything is under one roof and there are hundreds of shops where you can buy fresh fruits, vegetables, grains and much more. You can also go to one of the open-air street markets, called *ferias del agricultor*, on any Saturday morning. Farmers bring their fresh produce to these street markets each week, and you will find a variety of produce, meats and eggs at low prices.

A few words about Costa Rica's excellent seafood. With oceans on both sides, Costa Rica has a huge variety of fresh seafood. Tuna, dorado, corvina, abound as well as lobster, shrimp of all sizes and some crab. All of these can be purchased at any *pescadería* (fish market) in and around San José's Central Market at low prices. While you're there, try a heaping plate of *ceviche* (fish cocktail) at one of the many fish restaurants called *marisquerías*.

Typical Costa Rican food is similar to that of Mexico and other Central American countries. Tortillas often, but not always, are eaten with a meal of rice, beans, fruit, eggs, vegetables and a little meat. The most common dish, *gallo pinto*, is made from rice and black beans and fried with red bell peppers and cilantro. The *best gallo* pinto is served at La Soda Tapia restaurant opposite the Sabana Park in San José.

Some other popular Costa Rican foods include: *casado* (fish, chicken, or meat with beans and chopped cabbage), *empanadas* (a type of stuffed bread), *arreglados* (a kind of sandwich) and *palmito* (heart of palm), which is usually eaten separately or in salads.

MAJOR SUPERMARKETS

PERIFERICOS (several locations in the San José area)

MAS POR MENOS (largest chain)

AUTO MERCADOS (the best supermarkets in Costa Rica)

LA GRAN VIA (downtown San José)

BUBIS (specializing in expensive imported food products)

PALI SUPERMERCADOS (discount warehouses)

CENTRAL MARKET - MERCADO CENTRAL, located between Avenida Central and 1 and calle 6 and 8, has great food bargains.

RELIGION

Although 90% of Costa Ricans are Roman Catholic, there is freedom of religion and other religious views are permitted.

We hope the list of churches we have provided below will help you. Call the number of your denomination and you will be directed to your nearest house of worship in the San José area. There are some services in English in the San José area. (The asterisks denote churches where these special services in English are held).

* QUAKER 233-61-68
  UNITARIAN .... 228-10-20 or 228-41-96
  SYNAGOGUE SHAARE ZION (Jewish) 222-54-49
* B'NEI ISRAEL 225-85-61
  PROTESTANT 228-05-53
  UNION CHURCH 226-36-70
* MORMAN.. 234-19-45
  YOGA.. 221-58-95
  METHODIST 222-03-60
  CHRISTIAN SCIENCE 221-08-40
* BAPTIST (San Pedro) 253-79-11
* EPISCOPAL 222-15-60
* ESCAZU CHRISTIAN FELLOWSHIP 231-54-44
  JEHOVAH'S WITNESS 221-14-36
* SEVENTH DAY ADVENTISTS 223-77-59
  CATHOLIC (ESCAZU) 228-06-35
  CATHOLIC (LOS YOSES) 225-67-78
  CATHOLIC (ROHRMOSER) 232-21-28
  CATHOLIC (BARRIO SAN BOSCO) 221-37-48
  CATHOLIC (DOWNTOWN CATHEDRAL) 221-38-20
* VICTORY CHRISTIAN CENTER 282-77-20
* UNITY CHRIST INTERNATIONAL 228-68-05

HOLIDAYS IN COSTA RICA

Costa Ricans are very nationalistic and proudly celebrate their official holidays, called *feriados*. You should try to plan your activities around these holidays and not count on getting any important bureacratic matters or business done since most government and private offices will be closed. In fact, the whole country seems to shut down during *Semana Santa* (the week before Easter) and the week between Christmas and New Year's Day.

TRAPICHE - SUGAR MILL

January 1st	NEW YEAR'S DAY
March 19th	SAINT JOSEPH'S DAY
Holy Week	HOLY THURSDAY and GOOD FRIDAY
April 11th	JUAN SANTA MARIA'S DAY (local hero)
May 1st	LABOR DAY
May	UNIVERSITY WEEK
June	FATHER'S DAY (third Sunday)
July 25th	ANNEXATION OF GUANACASTE PROVINCE
August 2nd	VIRGIN OF LOS ANGELES DAY
August 15th	MOTHER'S DAY
September 15th	INDEPENDENCE DAY
October 12th	COLUMBUS DAY - Discovery of America
October 31st	HALLOWEEN
November 2nd	DAY OF THE DEAD
December 8th	IMMACULATE CONCEPTION
December 25th	CHRISTMAS
December 25th	FERIA DE ZAPOTE (December 25th to January 2nd)
December 25th	FIESTAS DEL FIN DEL AÑO

BRINGING YOUR PETS TO COSTA RICA

We did not forget those of you who have pets. There are procedures for bringing your pets into the country that require very little except patience, some paperwork and a small fee.

First, a registered veterinarian from your home town must certify that your pets are free of internal and external parasites. It is necessary that your pet's vaccinations be up to date against rabies, distemper, leptosporosis, hepatitis and parvovirus with the rabies vaccination within the last three years. Remember, all of these required documents are indispensable and must be certified also by the Costa Rican consulate nearest your home town.

Now if you should forget to comply with these regulations and not provide the required documents, your pet(s) can be refused entry, placed in quarantine or even put to sleep. But don't worry if worse come to worse there is a 30-day grace period to straighten things out.

If you ever want to take your pet out of Costa Rica you will have to get a special permit. You will also need a certificate from a local veterinarian and have all vaccinations up-to-date. Once you obtain these documents, you then have to go to the Ministry of Health, and your pet is free to leave the country.

Additional information and the requirements listed above are available through the Departamento de Zoonosis, Ministerio de Salud, Apartado Postal 10123, San José. Telephone 223-03-33, extension 331.

VETERINARIANS

Clinica Echandi 223-31-11
Dr. Federico Piza 248-71-66
Dr. Douglas Lutz 225-67-84
Dr. L. Starkey 253-71-42
Tecnologia Veterinaria (clinic, pharmacy, and boarding) 228-93-47
Dr. Lorena Guerra (comes to your home, also boarding) 228-98-87
For additional Veterinarians, look under the heading *"VETERINARIA"* in the yellow pages.

SERVICES FOR THE DISABLED AND HANDICAPPED

Getting around in the U.S. or Canada is hard enough when a person is disabled, let alone in a foreign country like Costa Rica.

Depending on the extent of the disability or handicap, disabled persons will find living in Costa Rica not much of an obstacle. There are not many facilities for disabled individuals and the terrain can sometimes be hard to negotiate. Some places have wheel chair access. A few hotels like the Grand Hotel Central America, are accessible to the handicapped because they are only one story high.

Keep in mind that taxis are inexpensive and the best way to travel for people with physical impediments. Since hired help is such a bargain, a full-time employee may be hired for companionship or as a nurse for a very reasonable price. In addition, medical care is relatively inexpensive in Costa Rica.

There is also a club for disabled veterans that meets once a month where they can socialize. Call 443-98-70 for more information.

We suggest that you pick up the book, "Access to the World: A Travel Guide For the Handicapped," by Louise Weiss, Published by Chatham Square Press, 401 Broadway, New York, NY 10013. This book contains good information and suggestions for disabled travelers.

UNDERSTANDING THE METRIC SYSTEM

If you plan to live in Costa Rica, it is in your best interest to understand the metric system. You will soon notice that automobile speedometers, road milage signs, the contents of bottles, and rulers are written in metric measurements. Since you probably didn't study this system when you were in school and it is almost never used in the U.S., you could become confused.

The conversion guide below will help you.

To Convert:	To:	Multiply by:
Centigrade	Farhenheit	1.8 then add 32
Square km	Square miles	0.3861
Square km	Acres	247.1
Meters	Yards	1.094
Meters	Feet	3.281
Liters	Pints	2.113
Liters	Gallons	0.2642
Kilometers	Miles	0.6214
Kilograms	Pounds	2.205
Hectares	Acres	2.471
Grams	Ounce	0.03527
Centimeter	Inches	0.3937

* Courtesy of *Costa Rica Today*.

CHAPTER TEN

Parting Thoughts
and Advice

10.

PERSONAL SAFETY IN COSTA RICA

While living in Costa Rica is much safer than residing in most large cities in the United States or most other Latin American countries, there are some precautions you should take to insure your own safety.

In Costa Rica the rate for violent crimes is very low compared to other places in the world, but there is a problem with petty theft, especially in the larger cities. Thieves tend to look for easy targets, especially foreigners, so you can't be too cautious. We recommend that you make sure your house or apartment has steel bars on both the windows and garage. The best bars are narrowly spaced, because some thieves have been known to use small children as accomplices because they can squeeze through the bars to burglarize your residence.

It is also a good idea to make sure your neighborhood has a night watchman if you live in the city. Some male domestic employees are willing to work in this capacity. However, you should ask for references and closely screen any person you hire. Also, report suspicious people who may be loitering around your premises. Thieves are very patient and will often case a residence for a long time to observe your comings and goings. They can and will strike at the most opportune moment.

You should take added precautions if you live in a neighborhood where there are a lot of foreigners. Thieves associate foreigners with wealth and look for areas where they are clustered together. One possible deterrent, in addition to a night watchman, is to organize some type of neighborhood watch group among the residents of your area. There are also private home security patrols that can provide an alarm system and patrol your area for a monthly fee. If you have to leave town it is a good idea to get a friend or some other trustworthy person to house sit while you are away.

If you are really concerned about protecting your valuables, you will be better off living in a condominium complex or an apartment. Both tend to be less susceptible to burglary due to their design and the fact that there is "safety in numbers," as the saying goes.

If you own an automobile, you should also be careful, especially if you have *pensionado* (retiree) license plates. These plates identify you as a foreigner and, in some cases, make you a sitting duck for car burglars who relish the opportunity to break into your car and steal your valuables. Make sure your house or apartment has a garage with iron bars so you won't have to park your car on the street. When parking away from your house, you should always park in parking lots or where there is a watchman. The latter will look after your car for a few cents an hour when you have to park it on the street. It is not difficult to find one of these people to watch your car since they will usually approach you and offer their services as soon as you park your car.

Pickpockets can be a problem. You should never flaunt your wealth by wearing expensive jewelry or carrying cameras loosely around you neck because they make you an easy mark on the street. It is advisable to find a good way to conceal your money, and never carry it in your back pocket. If you have to carry large amounts of money, use traveler's checks. You should also never carry any original documents, such as passports or visas. Make a photocopy of your passport and carry it with you at all times. The authorities will accept most photocopies as a valid form of identification. Men should also watch out for prostitutes, who often are expert pickpockets and can relieve you of your valuables before you realize it. Men, especially when inebriated or alone, should watch themselves at night in the vicinity of Morazán Park, The Holiday Inn and Key Largo Bar. There have been a lot of muggings reported in this area at night.

If you are a single woman living by yourself, you should never walk alone at night. If you do have to go out at night, be sure to take a taxi or have a friend go along.

There is some white collar crime in Costa Rica and always a few dishonest individuals-Americans, Canadians and Costa Ricans included--waiting to take your money. We have heard stories of naive foreigners loosing their hard-earned savings to ingenious con men's scams. So, be wary of "blue ribbon" business deals that seem too good to be true, or any other get-rich quick schemes. Most people you meet in Costa Rica will be honest, hard-working individuals. But don't assume people are honest just because they are nice. Again, it doesn't hurt to be overly cautious.

If you are robbed or swindled under any circumstances you should contact the police or in some cases the *O.I.J. (Organización de Investigacion Judicial)* a special highly efficient-investigative unit like the FBI (located between Aves 8 and 10 and Calles 15 and 17 in the middle court house, Tel: 255-01-22). You may also want to contact the Security Ministry, *Ministerio de Seguridad* at 224-48-66. By doing this you may not recover what has been stolen from you, but you may prevent others from being victimized in the future.

CONCLUSION

Throughout this book we have attempted to provide you with the most up-to-date information available on retirement and living in Costa Rica. We have also provided you with many useful suggestions to help make your life in Costa Rica more enjoyable and save you a lot of inconveniences. Adjusting to life in a new culture can prove rather difficult for some people. One of our aims is to make this transition easier, so you can take advantage of all the marvelous things that Costa Rica has to offer.

Before you move permanently to Costa Rica, we highly recommend you spend some time there on a trial basis to make sure it is the place for you. We are not talking about a few days or weeks, but a couple of months or even longer, so you can experience what Costa Rican life is really like. You should remember it is one thing to visit Costa Rica as a tourist and another thing to live there on a permanent basis. It is also best that you visit for extended periods during both the wet season, visit the dry season. That way you will get an idea of what the country is like at all times of the year. During your visits you should talk to many foreign retirees and gather as much information as possible before you make your final decision. It is a good idea to attend one of the Newcomer's Seminars held every Tuesday at the Hotel Irazú, except for the last Tuesday of each month when they are held at the Hotel Cariari. They are very informative. You will learn a lot by talking to other retirees and make some good contacts.

The final step, you might choose before deciding if you want to make Costa Rica your home, is to try living there for at least a year. This should be sufficient time to give you an idea of what long-term living in Costa Rica is really like and the kind of problems you may be confronted with while trying to adapt to living in a new culture. It should also afford you the opportunity to get acclimated to the climate and new foods. Hopefully, you should learn all the do's and don'ts, in's and out's and places to go or places to avoid during that period of time, before making your final decision.

After spending some time in Costa Rica, you may decide that you are not suited for full-time living there and perhaps want to try seasonal living for a few months a year. Many people spend the summer in the U.S. or Canada and winter in Costa Rica, which is their summer. This way they can enjoy the best of both worlds, or as they say, the endless summer. As we mentioned in Chapter 8, this is easy to do, since you can stay in the country up to six months legally as a tourist without having to get any type of permanent residency.

Whether you choose to reside in Costa Rica on a full or part-time basis, there are some things you should keep in mind regarding the cultural differences and new customs. First, life in Costa Rica is very different. If you expect all things to be exactly like they are in the United States, you are deceiving yourself. For example, the concept of time and punctuality is not important in Latin America. It is not unusual and not considered in bad taste for a person to arrive late for a business appointment or a dinner engagement. This custom can be incomprehensible and infuriating to the North American mentality. It will not change since it is a deeply rooted tradition. Also, as we previously mentioned, in most cases bureaucracy moves at a snail's pace in Costa Rica, which can be equally maddening to a foreigner. In addition, at times the Latin mentality, *machismo*, apparent illogical reasoning, traditions, different laws and ways of doing business, will seem incomprehensible to a naive foreigner.

There are countless other examples of different customs and cultural idiosyncrasies you will notice once you have lived in Costa Rica for a while. The best thing you can do is respect these different cultural values, be understanding and patient, and as they say "go with the flow." Learning Spanish will also benefit you.

Finally, we also reccommend that you shouldn't burn your bridges or sever your ties with your home country in the event you cannot adjust to life in Costa Rica and decide to return home.

Despite our efforts to constantly update this book, all of the aforementioned data may be subject to change at any given time. So, the authors urge you to be sure and check and see that our information is still accurate.

THANK YOU!

ADDITIONAL RETIREMENT INFORMATION

The *COSTA RICAN OUTLOOK* is an innovative, bi-monthly newsletter that covers a wide range of subjects and is packed with useful information about Costa Rica including an occasional article about retirement. They also offer insightful retirement trips to Costa Rica a couple of times a year. Reading this newsletter is another good way to keep abreast of what is happening in Costa Rica. You can subscribe for $19.00 a year if you live in the U.S. and $22.00 abroad. Write:

Costa Rican Outlook,
P.O. Box 5573
Chula Vista, CA 91912-5573,
Tel. 1-(800)365-2342, Fax (619) 421-6002

LA VOZ is published by the Costa Rican Resident's Association and not for sale to the general public. However, if you join the Pensionado Association your membership will include a monthly copy of their newsletter. For information:

Costa Rican Resident's Association
Apdo. Postal 700-1011
Y Griega, San José, Costa Rica
Central America.
Tel. (506) 233-80-68 & 233-10-17,Fax (506) 222-78-62

The *NEWCOMER'S SEMINAR* provides useful information at no charge. These weekly seminars are held each Tuesday at the Hotel Irazú, except on the last Tuesday of every month when they are held at the Hotel Cariari. For information: *The Newcomer's Seminar*, Box 962, San José, Costa Rica, Tel. (506) 232-13-55, Fax (506) 231-04-69

LIFESTYLE EXPLORATIONS has trips for prospective retirees to Costa Rica. To contact them write to:

Lifestyle Explorations
101 Federal Street, Suite 1900
Boston, MA 02110
Tel. (508) 371-4814, Fax (508) 369-9192

SUGGESTED READING

BOOKS

The New Key to Costa Rica, by Beatrice Blake. Ulysses Press, Berkeley, California. An excellent, easy to follow guide that is packed with useful information. We recommend it highly - a must for anyone visiting Costa Rica.

The Costa Rican Traveler, by Ellen Searby. Windham Bay Press, Box 1198, Occidental CA 95465. This book along with "The New Key to Costa Rica" are the two best guidebooks for tourists as well as locals. Also a 'must'.

The Adventure Guide to Costa Rica, by Harry S. Pariser, Hunter Publications, Edison, N.J. 08818. A straight forward easy-to-use guide. Another good guidebook.

The Essenstial Road Guide for Costa Rica, by Bill Baker. Apdo. 185-1011 San Jose, Costa Rica. A good guide book if you plan to do a lot of driving in the country. In the U.S. call 1-800-881-8607 or write to International Marketing Partners, Inc., 104 Half Moon Circle, H-3, Hypoluxo, Fl. 33462.

Costa Rica - A Travel Survival Kit, by Rob Rackowiecki. Lonely Planet Publications, Inc., P.O. 2001A, Berkeley, CA 94702. A good guide book.

Costa Rica, A Natural Destination, by Ree Strange Sheck. John Muir Publications, Santa Fe, NM. This book deals mostly with Costa Rica's natural wonders and ecology. Great for nature lovers.

Choose Costa Rica, by John Howells, Gateway Books, San Rafael, Ca. This book covers living in Costa Rica and has many interesting anecdotes, but fails to go into a lot of the negatives. It also lacks a lot of specifics about everyday life in Costa Rica.

The Costa Ricans, by Richard, Karen, and Mavis Biesanz. Waveland Press, Prospect Heights, IL.

Living in Costa Rica, by the U. S. Mission Association. A lot of excellent information, and a good reference book.

How You Can Avoid Losses Buying Costa Rican Real Estate, also by Bill Baker, 104 Half Moon Circle H-3, Hypoluxo, Fl. 33462. Another excellent publication by Mr. Baker that deals with the real estate market in Costa Rica and helps the reader develop a game plan for investing.

Insight Guide to Costa Rica, by Harvey Haber, distributed by Houghton Miflin and Prentice-Hall. Beautiful full-color guidebook.

Costa Rica, by Paul Glassman. Passport Press, Box 1346, Champlain, New York, 12919. A good guide with many maps.

Exploring Costa Rica, The Tico Times 1993-1994 Guide, This 200 page book is available through the *Tico Times* newspaper for $5.95. It contains a wealth of information about Costa Rica and is an excellent resource book.

Driving the Panamerican Highway to Mexico and Central America, by Raymond & Audrey Pritchard. Interlink 209, P.O. Box 526770, Miami, Fl. 33152. This is the only book available if you are planning to drive from the U.S. to Costa Rica via the Panamerican highway.

Happy Aging with Costa Rican Women - The Other Costa Rica, by James Kennedy, Box Canyon Books, Canoga Park, California.

Adventures Abroad, Exploring the Travel/Retirement Option, by Allene Symons and Jane Parker, Gateway Books, San Rafael, California, 1991. Good retirement tips for many countries including Costa Rica.

Purchasing Real Estate in Costa Rica, by Attorney Alvaro Carballo. Apartado 6997-1000, San José, Costa Rica. FAX: (506) 223-9151. This guide clears up a lot of misinformation and eases the anxiety of purchasing real estate in a foreign country.

Mexico and Central America Handbook. Distributed by Rand McNally. Not as detailed as books that deal specifically with Costa Rica.

South America Handbook. Published yearly by Rand McNally. General information for the traveler.

Central America on a Shoestring, by Geoff Crowther, Lonely Planet Publications, Australia. A necessity for the cost conscious traveler.

Frommer's Costa Rica, Guatemala and Belize on $35 a Day, Published by Prentice Hall Press, 1991. A good guide book for travelers.

SUGGESTED READING

A Costa Rican Guidebook, by Christopher D. Baker. Moon Publications; 700 pages. Due out in June of 1994.

PERIODICALS

Costa Rica Today Newspaper, published weekly. See page 54 for subscription details. This newspaper is more for tourists than the Tico Times, more colorful and pleasing to the eye.

The Tico Times Newspaper, Published weekly. See page 54 for subscription details. Not as upbeat as the competition, Costa Rica Today, but definately worth subscribing to if you are interested in living in Costa Rica.

Adventures in Costa Rica, is a newly published newsletter that is full of humorous anecdotes and some useful information. It is written by a couple who plan to retire in Costa Rica in a few years. Contact Starflame Publications, P.O. Box 508, Jackson, Ca. 95642. Tel: (209) 223-2771, or 296-5109. FAX: (209) 223-1588.

The Reach-Out Telephone Directory, co-sponsored by the Tico Times and AT&T. Ossuli, S.A., Apartado 6426-1000, San José, Costa Rica. Lists Services (doctors, taxis, dentists, etc.) in Costa Rica where English is spoken.

VIDEOS

*Travel Adventure Videos offer a 50-minute video called, "Costa Rica Adventures". This video gives a general overview of Costa Rica, and is a great introduction to the country if you have never been there before. Write: *Travel Adventure Videos,* P.O. Box 8474 Newport Beach, Ca. 92658 or call (714) 723-1122.

Costa Rica: Making the Most of Your Trip a 90 minute video. Megaview Productions, 831 Main St. Burbank, CA 91506

IMPORTANT SPANISH PHRASES AND VOCABULARY

You should know all of the vocabulary below if you plan to live in Costa Rica.

What's your name?	*¿ Cómo se llama usted?*
Hello!	*¡Hola!*
Good Morning	*Buenos días*
Good Afternoon	*Buenas tardes*
Good night	*Buenas noches*
How much is it?	*¿Cuánto es?*
How much is it worth?	*¿Cuánto vale?*
I like	*Me gusta*
You like	*Le gusta*
Where is...?	*¿Dónde está...?*
Help!	*¡Socorro!*
What's the rate of exchange	*¿Cuál es el tipo de cambio?*

I'm sick	*Estoy enfermo*	day after	
		tomorrow	*pasado mañana*
where	*dónde*	week	*la semana*
what	*qué*	Sunday	*domingo*
when	*cuándo*	Monday	*lunes*
how much	*cuánto*	Tuesday	*martes*
how	*cómo*	Wednesday	*miércoles*
which	*cuál or cuáles*	Thursday	*jueues*
why	*por qué*	Friday	*vienes*
		Saturday	*sábado*
now	*ahora*		
later	*más tarde*	month	*mes*
tomorrow	*mañana*	January	*enero*
tonight	*esta noche*	February	*febrero*
yesterday	*ayer*	March	*marzo*
day before		April	*abril*
yesterday	*anteaycr*	May	*mayo*

June	*junio*		short	*bajo*
July	*julio*		tired	*cansado*
August	*agosto*		bored	*aburrido*
September	*septiembre*		happy	*contento*
October	*octubre*		sad	*triste*
November	*noviembre*			
December	*diciembre*		expensive	*caro*
			cheap	*barato*
spring	*primavera*		more	*más*
summer	*verano*		less	*menos*
fall	*otoño*		inside	*adentro*
winter	*invierno*		outside	*afuera*
			good	*bueno*
north	*norte*		bad	*malo*
south	*sur*		slow	*lento*
east	*este*		fast	*rápido*
west	*oeste*		right	*correcto*
			wrong	*equivocado*
left	*izquierda*		full	*lleno*
right	*derecha*		empty	*vacío*
easy	*fácil*		early	*temprano*
difficult	*difícil*		late	*tarde*
big	*grande*		best	*el mejor*
small	*pequeño, chiquito*		worst	*el peor*
a lot	*mucho*		I understand	*comprendo*
a little	*poco*		I don't	
there	*allí*		understand	*no comprendo*
here	*aquí*		Do you speak	
nice, pretty	*bonito*		English?	*¿Habla usted inglés?*
ugly	*feo*			
old	*viejo*		hurry up!	*¡apúrese!*
young	*joven*		O.K.	*está bien*
fat	*gordo*		excuse me!	*¡perdón!*
thin	*delgado*		Watch out!	*¡cuidado!*
tall	*alto*			

143

open	*abierto*	bill	*la cuenta*
closed	*cerrado*		
occupied		blue	*azul*
(in use)	*ocupado*	green	*verde*
free (no cost)	*gratis*	black	*negro*
against the		white	*blanco*
rules or law	*prohibido*	red	*rojo*
exit	*la salida*	yellow	*amarillo*
entrance	*la entrada*	pink	*rosado*
stop	*alto*	orange	*anaranjado*
		brown	*café, castaño*
breakfast	*el desayuno*	purple	*morado,*
lunch	*el almuerzo*		*púrpura*
dinner	*la cena*		
cabin	*la cabina*	0	*cero*
bag	*la bolsa*	1	*uno*
sugar	*el azúcar*	2	*dos*
water	*el agua*	3	*trés*
coffee	*el café*	4	*cuatro*
street	*la calle*	5	*cinco*
avenue	*la avenida*	6	*seis*
beer	*la cerveza*	7	*siete*
market	*el mercado*	8	*ocho*
ranch	*la finca*	9	*nueve*
doctor	*el médico*	10	*diez*
egg	*el huevo*	11	*once*
bread	*el pan*	12	*doce*
meat	*el carne*	13	*trece*
milk	*la leche*	14	*catorce*
fish	*el pescado*	15	*quince*
ice cream	*el helado*	16	*diez y seis*
salt	*la sal*	17	*diez y siete*
pepper	*la pimienta*	18	*diez y ocho*
post office	*el correo*	19	*diez y nueve*
passport	*pasaporte*	20	*veinte*
waiter	*el salonero*	30	*treinta*

40	*cuarenta*	400	*cuatrocientos*
50	*cincuenta*	500	*quinientos*
60	*sesenta*	600	*seiscientos*
70	*setenta*	700	*setecientos*
80	*ochenta*	800	*ochocientos*
90	*noventa*	900	*novecientos*
100	*cien*	1000	*mil*
200	*doscientos*	1,000,000	*un millón*
300	*trescientos*		

* If you want to perfect your Spanish, we suggest you purchase our best-selling Spanish book, "**The Costa Rican Spanish Survival Course**", and 90-minute cassette mentioned in Chapter 3. It is a one-of-a-kind pocket-sized course designed for people who want to learn to speak Spanish the Costa Rican way.

TIQUISMOS

Here are some Costa Rican expressions you should be familiar with if you plan to spend a lot of time in Costa Rica.

birra	**beer**	*macho*	**blond haired person**
boca	**snack**	*maje*	**pal**
¡Bueno Nota!	**Fantastic, great**	*pachanga*	**party**
campo	**space (on a bus)**	*paja*	**B.S.**
chapa	**a coin or stupid person**	*pinche*	**a tightfisted person**
		pulpería	**corner grocery store**
Chepe	**slang for San José**	*queque*	**cake**
chicha	**anger**	*roco*	**old person**
chunche	**a thing**	*¡Salado!*	**Too bad! Tough luck!**
dar pelota	**flirt**	*soda*	**a small cafe**
fila	**line**	*Tico*	**A Costa Rican**
gato	**blue-eyed person**	*timba*	**big stomach**
goma	**hangover**	*tiquicia*	**Costa Rica**
harina	**money**	*vino*	**snoopy person**
jalar una torta	**get in trouble**	*vos*	**you, informal**
¡Jale!	**Hurry up!**		**equivalent of tú**

* There are hundreds more Costa Rican expressions. The ones above are some of the most frequently used.

INDEX

NOTES

NOTES

NOTES